Talk It Out!

The Educator's Guide to Successful Difficult Conversations

Barbara E. Sanderson, Ph.D.

EYE ON EDUCATION
6 DEPOT WAY WEST, SUITE 106
LARCHMONT, NY 10538
(914) 833-0551
(914) 833-0761 fax
www.eyeoneducation.com

Library of Congress Cataloging-in-Publication Data

Sanderson, Barbara E.
    Talk it out! : the educator's guide to successful difficult conversations
/ Barbara E. Sanderson.
        p. cm.
    ISBN 1-59667-008-8
    1. Communication in education. 2. Interpersonal communication.
3. Teachers--Professional relationships. 4. Conflict management.
I. Title.
LB1033.5.S28 2005
371.102'2--dc22

                                                2005015719

Editorial services and production provided by
UB Communications, 10 Lodge Lane, Parsippany, NJ 07054
(973) 331-9391

Also available from Eye On Education

What Great Principals Do Differently:
15 Things That Matter Most
Todd Whitaker

What Successful Principals Do!
169 Tips for Principals
Franzy Fleck

BRAVO Principal!
Sandra Harris

The Administrator's Guide to
School Community Relations, Second Edition
George E. Pawlas

Making the Right Decisions:
A Guide for School Leaders
Douglas J. Fiore and Chip Joseph

Stepping Outside Your Comfort Zone:
Lessons for School Leaders
Nelson Beaudoin

Dealing with Difficult Teachers, Second Edition
Todd Whitaker

Dealing with Difficult Parents
(And with Parents in Difficult Situations)
Todd Whitaker and Douglas Fiore

Great Quotes for Great Educators
Todd Whitaker and Dale Lumpa

What Great Teachers Do Differently:
14 Things That Matter Most
Todd Whitaker

20 Strategies for
Collaborative School Leaders
Jane Clark Lindle

Motivating & Inspiring Teachers
The Educational Leader's Guide for Building Staff Morale
Todd Whitaker, Beth Whitaker, and Dale Lumpa

Harnessing the Power of Resistance:
A Guide for Educators
Jared Scherz

The Principal as Instructional Leader:
A Handbook for Supervisors
Sally J. Zepeda

Instructional Leadership for School Improvement
Sally J. Zepeda

Six Types of Teachers: Recruiting, Retaining, and
Mentoring the Best
Douglas J. Fiore and Todd Whitaker

Supervision Across the Content Areas
Sally J. Zepeda and R. Stewart Mayers

The ISLLC Standards in Action:
A Principal's Handbook
Carol Engler

101 Answers for New Teachers and Their Mentors:
Effective Teaching Tips for Daily Classroom Use
Annette L. Breaux

Data Analysis for Continuous School Improvement
Victoria L. Bernhardt

School Leader Internship: Developing, Monitoring,
and Evaluating Your Leadership Experience
Gary Martin, William Wright, and Arnold Danzig

Handbook on Teacher Evaluation:
Assessing and Improving Performance
James Stronge & Pamela Tucker

Handbook on Teacher Portfolios
for Evaluation and Professional Development
Pamela Tucker & James Stronge

Acknowledgements

This book is dedicated to Angeles Arrien, who has been both a teacher and mentor to me. I feel deep gratitude for her wisdom, her profound compassion for everyone she meets, her consistent modeling of what she teaches, and her willingness to challenge me and to tell me the truth. Chapter Two of this book highlights some of what I have learned from her and her influence is manifest throughout the book.

I am also appreciative of two other powerful teachers, Patrick O'Neill and Tricia Mageli-Maley. They have helped me to grow and develop as a leader and as a person. I also want to acknowledge two mentors who provided me with a great deal of assistance in my Michigan days and are no longer with us, Walt Jenvey and Ed Pierce. When I was a university undergraduate, Gladys Beckwith started me on the road to understanding human communications, and I am forever grateful to her for doing so.

I have had the privilege of working with many wonderful educators as a consultant and as a colleague. Thank you for letting me share your journey. I have learned so much from you.

Thank you to Bob Sickles of Eye on Education for inviting me to write this book. He has been a joy to work with and has made the process easy for me.

I could not have written this book without Sue Wilson. She is my first and best editor and the chief encourager of everything I do in the world.

I am indebted for inspiration to directors Robert Robinson and Sandy Hodges, and all of the members of the choir in which I joyfully sing. I am also grateful for the support of many other colleagues and friends, including Lee Eddison, Patricia Falls, Sandy McElrath, Marcie New, Sharon O'Toole, Marg Penn, and Zhuoling Ren.

Barbara Sanderson
Thriving Workplaces
Minnetonka, Minnesota

Meet the Author

Barbara E. Sanderson, Ph.D., is the Executive Director of Thriving Workplaces: Helping Individuals and Organizations to Flourish. Dr. Sanderson is a psychologist, organizational consultant, executive coach, keynote speaker, and workshop leader. She has more than thirty years of in-depth experience working with individuals and organizations in the fields of education, health, mental health, religion, and business. Dr. Sanderson is also experienced as a teacher, administrator, employee assistance counselor, and facilitator.

Barbara Sanderson excels in developing collaborative relationships that are empowering, practical, and action-oriented. She has a proven ability to synthesize information and communicate clearly. Her strong leadership style utilizes integrity, compassion, insight, creativity, and humor. A few of the workplace topics on which she consults are

- ♦ Resolving conflict
- ♦ Building an environment of trust
- ♦ Welcoming and incorporating diversity
- ♦ Invoking personal leadership and self-responsibility
- ♦ Building teams and organization
- ♦ Successfully changing leaders
- ♦ Creating positive shifts in toxic work environments
- ♦ Learning to have difficult conversations

If you would like more information about Barbara Sanderson or would like to invite her to work with your group, please contact her in Minnesota.

www.thrivingworkplaces.com
Barbara@thrivingworkplaces.com
(952) 939-0456

Table of Contents

SECTION ONE

INTRODUCTION

Chapter 1

Why Difficult Conversations Are So Important

Estelle was an elementary teacher for 31 years and worked with five principals. Every year, Estelle had what she came to think of as "The Conversation" with her current principal. The principal would seek her out and say, "Estelle, people are really offended and put off by your comments in staff meetings," or words to that effect. Estelle prided herself on speaking the truth and often articulated what others avoided saying. She assumed that her principals meant that the content of her observations was unpleasant for people to hear and thought they were just too cowardly to say what-was-what themselves. Being someone who believed that strong medicine is good for you, she continued to speak her mind.

When Estelle retired, she decided that she would devote her resources to herself for the first time in her life. She attended workshops, learned to meditate, and participated in personal growth groups. In the process, she received feedback about her impact, positive and negative. Soon, she came to a new understanding about "The Conversation." "The content was never the problem, it was the way I delivered my messages. I have been sarcastic, shaming, blaming, judgmental, and condescending without realizing it. It's no wonder people ducked every time I opened my mouth. I'm excited that I understand the problem—now I can do something about it. I'm also sad because I realize that many of my insights were lost."

This is a story about failed difficult conversations. Estelle was insightful and gutsy, but lethal in her communication style, so her conversations were not successful. Every year, her principal had the opportunity to give her specific feedback about her behavior and its impact, which could have helped her to correct her course. Instead, she received comments that were so general that they were useless. She made inaccurate assumptions about what the principals meant and continued on in her destructive pattern.

The fallout from these missed communications was considerable. Estelle's sharp tongue helped to create a lack of safety in 31 years of staff meetings. Many of her colleagues stopped speaking up because they didn't want to get roasted. Her principals felt weak and ineffective in their efforts to try to modify Estelle's behavior and didn't understand why they were never successful. Many staff members blamed the principals for not reining her in at staff meetings. Estelle was not able to bring her considerable gifts and talents fully to the table because her own negative communication style sabotaged her efforts. Her style also cost her strong working relationships with people for whom she had genuine respect and caring.

What Is a Difficult Conversation?

A difficult conversation is one that requires courage on the part of one or both parties. It may be challenging to initiate the conversation, to receive it, or both. You may get weak in the knees at the thought of initiating a difficult conversation, or you may observe this reaction in others when they are on the receiving end. Even though you may find such a conversation to be non-threatening, that doesn't necessarily mean that the other person isn't challenged.

A *successful* difficult conversation also requires that the message be delivered in a way that others can hear. Content, timing, and tone of voice are all important. What it takes to succeed is a combination of courage and skills.

The purpose of a difficult conversation is to clear the air and to find resolutions to situations that are bothersome to you. The goal is not to triumph over the other party, but to work together to find mutually satisfying, win/win solutions.

At work, we have connections with all of our colleagues. Having a positive, constructive work relationship does not require that we like the other person. It does mean that we have clear, open communication with each other. It is possible to value a work relationship without wanting the other person to become a close personal friend.

A whole host of circumstances may trigger the need for a difficult conversation. You might dislike the way you've been treated. You may feel let down by someone who did not deliver what was promised. You might want to know where you stand with someone. You may feel that your values are being compromised. You might need to own up to a mistake by making amends. You might need to address the behavior or performance problems of a colleague or supervisee. Or, as the comedian Flip Wilson used to say, someone may be "on your very last nerve."

If It's So Difficult, Why Do It?

There are three compelling reasons to have courageous conversations at work. First, it is impossible to create an environment of trust without risking speaking your truth. Second, if you do not express matters that concern you, it will add to your level of stress. Third, when you don't say what's on your mind, your sense of personal sufficiency suffers.

Creating an Atmosphere of Trust

Would you like to have a more trusting environment in your workplace? There is no mystery about how to create trust: it is achieved by the sum of the behavior choices of all of the members of the group. Each minute of the day, you get to choose whether your behavior will add to or subtract from the level of trust in your organization. The more your actions contribute to a sense of reliability, integrity, and dependability, the more you will trust yourself, others, and the organization.

Bryk and Schneider (2002)*, in their longitudinal research in the Chicago schools, found that the trust among the adults in schools—teachers, parents, and administrators—was a key factor in successful school reform and in improving student academic achievement. They reported four contributors to such trust: respect, personal regard for others, competence, and personal integrity.

Respect allows people to disagree while still valuing each other. Personal regard is created when people extend themselves beyond what is expected. When those in leadership positions do not address incompetence, trust is eroded in the group. Personal integrity comes from an internal moral compass that keeps actions in alignment with words and puts the welfare of students first. All four of these aspects of trust require the ability to have successful difficult conversations.

Trust is a prerequisite for creativity and learning. It creates a rich environment that nourishes everyone's gifts and helps them to bring their talents forward. Without it, vital energy is dissipated in discontent and frustration. Without trust, tasks are not accomplished in the easiest and most fulfilling ways, and relationships become strained and then falter. Good people are unhappy and less productive.

> Ron was a high school physics teacher. He had worked in the same school for 10 years under three principals. During that time, the atmosphere in the building had deteriorated

---

* Bryk, Anthony S., and Schneider, Barbara (2002). *Trust in Schools: A Core Resource for Improvement*. New York: Russell Sage Foundation.

markedly into backbiting, gossip, and negativity. Sometimes he felt that he had to drag himself to school in the morning. To his colleagues, Ron complained frequently and loudly about the size of his classes, other teachers who were not pulling their weight, disrespectful students, interfering parents, and the decisions of the school board. Most of all, he complained about the principal, whom he blamed for the negative working environment.

One morning, Ron made his usual complaints to a new substitute, who looked at him and said, "And what's your part? What are you doing to make the environment here more positive?" Ron didn't have an answer, but the questions stuck with him. He started paying attention to his own behavior and what it produced. He noticed that his fault-finding left him feeling worn out and empty, and he decided to experiment with dropping the behavior. Within a week, he felt more energetic, and a month later he felt a renewed passion for teaching. He reported, "I feel good about this place again. It's strange, because the only thing that's changed is me. There are still real problems, but how I'm interacting with them is different."

The ability to create trust begins with trusting yourself. There is a tendency to look at other people's behavior when you think trust is lacking. There is very little that you can do to change the behavior of others; the only thing you can do is change your own behavior. If you decide to become more trustworthy and stick to it, others will likely be inspired by your example and join you. Simply pointing a finger at the unproductive behaviors of others will only decrease the level of trust in your organization. Start by looking in the mirror.

You create trust when you are curious about yourself, rather than self-bullying—i.e., when you are feeling sufficient. You generate confidence when you take responsibility for your actions and your impact on others. When you are willing to look again, and not just be positional, you become more reliable.

Creating openings for others, rather than comparing yourself to them, builds confidence. Checking assumptions before you act on them instills trust. Identifying with what's working and not succumbing to negativity begets trust. Grounding your work in your passion, rather than looking outside of yourself for direction and meaning, is inspiring to others.

When you have a reaction to something and you say what is true for you without blaming, shaming, or judging the other person, you create a wealth of trust. You bank even more trust if you deliver the message within a week, set the context for the content, and are very specific. If you choose to tell a third party, instead of going directly to the person with whom you have a problem, you create an unproductive triangle and erode the trust in the group. The same thing happens if you withdraw or attempt to appease the other person.

When you are able to trust, you can let go of the outcome (once you have done your best) rather than trying to control others to get what you want. Letting go will allow you to put closure to things that are in the past, accept reality, and prevent you from trying to rescue or fix others.

Reducing Stress

When something is bugging you, it's hard to set it down. Even if you try to put it out of your mind, it pops back up again. If that something is a problem between you and someone with whom you work, it can become a daily irritant. Gathering your courage and talking about the problem without blame or judgment is a way to set it down.

If you keep the problem to yourself or complain to a third party, you make the problem worse and contribute to your own level of stress. If you are carrying around many unspoken difficult conversations, then your stress level is probably high. In the extreme, bottling up your anger and frustration can lead to clinical depression and anxiety and physical health problems. People who dare to speak up in a constructive way report an immediate lowering of their feelings of stress.

> Terry was a middle-school media specialist who prided herself in collaborative working relationships with teachers. Bob, a veteran social studies teacher, regularly brought his students to the media center to work on special projects.

Unlike other teachers, when he brought his students to the center, Bob didn't stay with them, but left and went to the teachers' lounge. Each time he left, Terry smoldered inside, but she didn't say anything to him. When Terry found herself having trouble getting to sleep because she felt so angry with Bob, she decided to risk having a talk with him.

The next time Bob's class came into the media center, Terry felt her heart speed up and her mouth go dry. She wiped her clammy palms and approached Bob for a difficult conversation. Afterwards, she reported, "After I got the first sentence out of my mouth, I calmed down. My heart stopped racing, and it wasn't nearly as hard as I'd imagined it would be. I slept much better that night."

As you think about approaching someone to have a difficult conversation, you may have a physiological response: dry mouth, shaking hands or knees, cart-wheeling stomach, sweating palms or pits, racing heart. These sensations are normal and mean that you are about to do something important. They are like a neon arrow with a sign that says, "YOU'RE IN THE RIGHT PLACE: DIG HERE." It is possible to mistake these physical reactions as a bodily warning to stop or flee. Instead, they are actually a sign that you are doing exactly what you need to do.

Building Self-esteem

Every time you have the courage to speak what's on your mind in a constructive way, you build your self-esteem. Conversely, when you clam up when something is bothering you, you take your self-worth down a notch. It's a very simple formula. One of the best ways to build your self-esteem is to bravely find your voice.

You feel good about yourself when you are courageous, and you feel bad about yourself when you are not. Your character, who you are at the core, wants you to be strong-hearted. When you violate that inner knowing, it is easy to slip into shame and self-loathing. The more you work against yourself, the lower your sense of sufficiency becomes. The more insufficient you feel, the less reliable you become to yourself and to others. Your trust in yourself is eroded.

At the end of her first year of teaching middle school math, Sondra was feeling low. There was so much about teaching that still seemed to elude her. She hadn't been able to figure out how to teach fractions so that all of her students could understand. Her fourth and fifth period classes had sometimes degenerated into chaos because of her lack of classroom management skills. She had spent almost every evening and most of her weekends working on her lesson plans and grading papers, and yet she still felt that she was lagging behind. She wondered if she was really sharp enough to be a teacher.

That summer, Sondra did something that had been a dream of hers—she learned how to fly-fish. Near the end of her second day of drifting and casting for trout, Sondra repeatedly snarled her line around her pole and had to reach it back to the fishing guide to be untangled. When she did this for the fifth time in a row, she mumbled to the guide, "I'm sorry. I'm such an idiot."

The guide's head snapped up and he said, "There is nothing here to apologize for—you're in a steep learning curve. You can't get good without making lots of mistakes."

As the guide's admonitions soaked in, Sondra realized that his words also applied to her first year of teaching. She had been in a steep learning curve; she had made lots of mistakes and was a much better teacher than she had been at the beginning of the year. Sondra decided it was time to stop beating up on herself.

When you become highly self-critical, it is much more difficult to hear the still, small voice inside that is an accurate reflection of reality. The pull of irrationality becomes stronger. When you are in an unreliable state and someone misbehaves around you, you tend to believe it is about you, instead of mentally shaking your head and saying to yourself, "There he goes again—I wonder what that's about." Very little of others' behavior is actually about us, but lack of self-worth makes us believe that it is.

When we take things personally, we are in a reactive mode. Our emotional reflexes are quick and inaccurate. We leave people wondering, "What the heck just happened?" We don't feel good about ourselves and blame our feelings on others. We feel like victims and don't realize that our own reactivity has set up the dynamic. Rather than being curious about ourselves and others, we are judgmental. It is much more difficult to be proactive and self-responsible when we are reactive.

Insufficiency also gets in the way of our receiving feedback from others. If we believe that we are insignificant, information about our impact on others, positive or negative, is difficult to incorporate. Not having a feedback loop makes it hard to correct course when we are wobbling off track and also prevents us from hearing and believing laudatory input.

Ironically, low self-esteem makes it more likely that we will seek approval outside of ourselves. We want feedback, but when we get it, we cannot use it. Attention-seeking behavior escalates because we can never get enough approval.

Building sufficiency helps to inoculate us against taking things personally, being impervious to feedback, seeking approval and attention in unproductive ways, and being reactive. It assists us in staying curious, rather than moving into judgment against ourselves and others. Having successful, difficult conversations is one of the most powerful ways to build self-esteem.

It is imperative that each person in an organization is heard. You have a unique perspective, based on your gifts and talents and your life experiences and challenges. No one can replace your voice. You must dare to speak to bring forth your perspective.

What Is the Purpose of This Book?

This book is intended to help the adults who work in educational settings to acquire the skills and confidence necessary to have successful difficult conversations with each other. While the main thrust of this book is adult-to-adult interactions, the principles taught here also apply to working with students.

The insights in this book are based on the author's experiences in over 35 years of professional life as a teacher, administrator, psychologist, employee assistance counselor, organizational consultant, and executive coach. The examples are drawn from her own experiences and from those of her friends, colleagues, and clients. In all cases, the names and identities in the stories have been changed to protect the confidentiality of individuals and organizations.

This book contains three sections. Chapter Two completes the introductory section and presents an overview of difficult conversations from a cross-cultural perspective.

The three chapters in the second section of the book examine some of the most pervasive roots of conflict in the workplace. Chapter Three explores problems related to task and to relationship. Chapters Four and Five present the roles of villain, victim, and rescuer and how they combine to form unproductive triangles in the workplace.

The third and final section of the book takes you through the process of difficult conversations. Chapter Six shows you how to prepare for a difficult conversation, and in Chapter Seven you learn how to initiate and have the conversation. Chapter Eight helps you to change tactics when you do not get the response that you want in challenging communications, and it helps you to respond when someone else approaches you with difficult material. Chapter Nine explores the challenges of power differentials between the two parties in the conversation. Chapter Ten weaves together the various strands of the book.

Chapter 2

A Cross-Cultural View of Difficult Conversations

No matter what world we live in now, we are all people of the earth, connected to one another by our mutual humanity. When we listen to land-based peoples, we are listening to our oldest selves. Indigenous cultures support change and healing, transition and rites of passage, through mythic structures and through the incorporation into daily life of art, science, music, ritual, and drama. Every culture in the world has singing, dancing, and storytelling, and these are practices to which we all have access. We also have access to the four archetypes, or blueprints for human behavior, which are present in the mythic structure of societies all over the world.

—Angeles Arrien, Ph.D., Anthropologist
The Four-Fold Way™*

---

* Arrien, Angeles (1993). *The Four-Fold Way: Walking the Paths of the Warrior, Teacher, Healer and Visionary.* San Francisco: Harper.

13

The wisdom in the four universal archetypes identified by Arrien can serve as a cross-cultural outline of the process for successful difficult conversations. The archetype of the warrior or leader demands that we first "choose to be present." The healer archetype counsels us to "pay attention to what has heart and meaning." The visionary archetype urges that we "tell the truth without blame or judgment." The archetype of the teacher advises that we "be open to outcome, not attached to outcome." Let's examine each one of these universal principles as it relates to challenging communications.

Choose to Be Present

We all have available a great source of individual power in our personal presence. When we are fully present, we are visible and people know where we stand on important issues. Our communications are clear and delivered at appropriate times with attention to tone and nonverbal impact. We are able to bring our gifts and talents into the world in satisfying ways. Being present is an act of respect toward ourselves and others. It helps us to work well with others.

When we are not present, we do not feel personally powerful. This sense of powerlessness may lead us to clash with those whom we do perceive as powerful. We may become rebels and try to make our mark by going against the established norms, oblivious to our negative impact on our colleagues and our workplaces. We may act in ways that are disrespectful to the rights and boundaries of others. When we are not present, we also may have a tendency to challenge authority in unproductive ways or to be fiercely independent. We may find it difficult to be part of a team.

There are four ways that we can be present: physically, mentally, emotionally, and spiritually. Each one of these forms of being present is important in successful difficult conversations.

Physical Presence

Most successful difficult conversations happen in person. It is an act of bravery to put your body in the room, ready to become a part of the solution to the problem at hand. Sometimes fear can be so overwhelming that we can't bring ourselves to show up.

> Sara had been teaching high school health for 34 years when the school board added sex education to the health curriculum. Sara had never had a sexual relationship and had managed to avoid even having a conversation about the issue with anyone. The thought of discussing sex with teenagers was terrifying. She felt too embarrassed to discuss her feelings with her principal beyond saying, "I can't do it."
>
> As the spring date for the start of sex education approached, Sara, who had not missed a day of teaching in her career, decided to ruin her perfect attendance record. She called for a substitute for the two weeks of the unit. This was a pattern that Sara repeated every year until she retired.
>
> Sara was a skillful teacher of other health topics, and she was generally well liked by students; however, once her students realized that she couldn't handle teaching them about sex, their respect for her eroded. They also knew how to fluster her—she frequently found condoms tucked into her desk drawers, and the color draining from her face was a gratifying result for her student pranksters.

Sara's story illustrates the power of physical presence—showing up, even when we are frightened. When we do the difficult things, we engender far more respect than when we do old and familiar things. It is better to muddle through something challenging than to avoid it altogether. Having a difficult conversation is a messy process. It requires courage, and people respect us for showing up. We also feel much better about ourselves when we take the risk. Bravery nourishes character, trust, and self-esteem.

Mental Presence

Being mentally present requires that we have our minds on what is happening in the moment. When we are mentally present, we are not processing past events, and we are not silently planning for the future. We do not have an unspoken agenda that we are working; instead, we are available to flow with discussion and to engage in creative collaboration.

Most sports require a high level of mental presence. Dragon boat racing, the fastest growing water sport in the world, is a good example. Dragon boats are 40 or more feet long and have a dragon's head at the bow and a dragon's tail on the stern. Eighteen paddlers, sitting two abreast, are so close together, front to back, that they must paddle in complete unison. If one paddler gets out of rhythm, he will smash his paddle into the paddles of the crew members seated in front and behind him, which will cause the boat to lose speed. In racing heats, the teams paddle flat out for approximately a minute and a half. Staying in unison requires intense focus on the part of each paddler. Before each heat, the captain calls, "Heads in the boat!" to remind the crew to use their mental presence. The crew's ability to focus is as important to winning the race as their physical strength.

Similarly, the mental presence of each staff member helps organizational events to flow smoothly. In meetings, being mentally present means that we are focused on whoever is speaking. It may be clear that being involved intellectually means that we are not thinking about what we will have for dinner or how to pick up the dry-cleaning and still get the children from day care on time. What is not so obvious is that being present mentally also means that we are not planning what we are going to say next while others are speaking. Staying mentally present requires that we trust ourselves to be able to muster our thoughts when it is our turn to speak.

In conversations, we have different impacts on other people, depending on whether we are mentally present or not. When we have our minds focused on other people, we are more likely to hear and understand what others are saying. When our thoughts are elsewhere, it is difficult to connect with other people, and it is more likely that they will walk away feeling frustrated and unheard. Responsiveness depends on mental presence.

Emotional Presence

There are two aspects to being emotionally present. One makes us aware of our own emotional reactions, and the other provides us with insights into the behavior of others.

When I have an awareness of my own emotions, I know what I am feeling. I can read the subtle nuances of my own inner reactions. If I have had a significant loss, I grieve. If I feel peaceful inside, I don't mistake that feeling for boredom. I know when I am feeling shy and can evaluate whether I want to encounter people or avoid them.

Being emotionally present allows me to be responsible for my feelings. I know when I am angry, with whom I am angry, and what has provoked me. With this knowledge, I can have a difficult conversation with the right person. I can express my anger cleanly and directly.

If I am not aware that I am angry or have not focused it on the correct person, then I am likely to behave in irresponsible ways. I may snarl at everyone in sight or indulge in blaming and shaming. If I am actually angry with myself, but am not aware of it, I am particularly vulnerable to smearing my feelings all over other people.

Being emotionally present gives me the opportunity to take responsibility for my feelings and how I act on them. Whatever I feel is acceptable. My actions based on those feelings may or may not be productive. I have a chance to choose when I am emotionally present.

> Jeanette was a middle school Spanish teacher. At the beginning of every school year, she took a large brooch from her desk and showed it to each class. "This is a crab. You will only see it four or five times this year. When I wear it, you will know that I am really crabby. If you mess with me when I have it on, you'll get a reaction you won't like."

Jeanette was savvy enough to know that there would be times during the year when she was less reliable emotionally. She might be coming down with a cold, she might have had a fight with her husband or her children, or she might be feeling overwhelmed by her mother's Alzheimer's disease. Whatever it turned out to be, she would be aware of it and would not want to take it out on her students. She would pin on the crab and give her students a warning to tread carefully.

When I take responsibility for my own emotions, it also makes it easier for me to tune in to the feelings of others. I am more aware when there is a shift in the emotional atmosphere. I may not know what the change means, but I'm aware enough to ask a question: "You don't seem to be your usually springy self this week—what's up?" Or I might suggest, "All of a sudden, things are feeling tense in this meeting. Let's stop and figure out what's happening."

Without the ability to tune in to the emotional state of others, it is difficult to be a good leader. I miss cues that indicate when people are excited and want to go further, or indications that the group is frustrated and has had enough. I can't surf the circumstances.

Classroom management is also more challenging when I am not emotionally present. It may be difficult to tell the difference between playfulness and disrespect. I may not know whether unusual behavior needs sympathy and reassurance or discipline. I may not know when a child needs help.

> Malcolm was in his second year as a third grade teacher when he frantically sought out Megan, the school social worker. "I'm freaked out! You know Eddie in my class—he's usually pretty quiet and a hard worker—actually, he's one of my favorite students. This week he's been acting different. First, he was really quiet. Then, today, he was hitting other kids and talking back to me. I had this tremendous urge to hit him! I didn't do it, and I've never hit anyone before! I've never even wanted to hit anyone! What's happening to me?"
>
> Megan asked, "Do you know if Eddie is being physically abused—is someone hitting him?" Malcolm responded, "I've never thought so. What makes you think that might be true?" Megan replied, "Sometimes when kids are abused, they learn subtle behaviors that bring out violent urges in others. If they don't get help, it sets them up to be abused throughout their lives. Your wanting to hit Eddie doesn't mean anything about you, except that you have sensitive radar for kids who have been traumatized. Let's talk to Eddie and try to make it safe for him to tell us about what's bothering him."

When Megan and Malcolm talked with Eddie privately, he revealed several years of physical abuse by his mother's boyfriend. The abuse had recently become worse when the boyfriend moved in with Eddie and his mother.

Malcolm received this valuable clue about Eddie's abuse because Malcolm was emotionally present with himself and with his students. Eddie got the help he needed because Malcolm was brave enough to risk sharing his powerful emotional reaction with Megan.

Spiritual Presence

Spiritual presence is not about religion. It is an awareness of our true nature. Arrien notes that, at the core, we are all "good, true, and beautiful." When I am spiritually present, I remember that I am good, true and beautiful and so is everyone else with whom I come into contact. Regardless of how other people are behaving, I can reach for the best in them if I am spiritually present.

When people are misbehaving, it is tempting to respond in kind. If they are angry, it is easy to be angry back. It takes personal discipline to be compassionate while holding people accountable for their behavior. When you are faced with provocative behavior, you must stay solidly spiritually present not to respond too harshly.

As a master teacher, Paul spent part of his day running an elementary math lab and the other portion mentoring probationary teachers. Paul happened to be in the school parking lot one fall afternoon when an angry father accosted Tony, one of his mentees. A loud, angry exchange ensued. When it was over and the parent had screeched out of the lot, Paul followed Tony back into the building.

Paul put a hand on Tony's shoulder and said, "That looked pretty tough."

Tony, still shaking, replied, "That jerk! He had the nerve to come here and yell at me because his son flunked a math test. He accused me of being an incompetent teacher. He wouldn't even listen to what I had to say. The truth is, his son never does his homework, and he talks and makes trouble during class. I lost it and started yelling back at him. I told him that he was an incompetent parent who had produced an irresponsible, disrespectful son. I said it was no wonder his kid behaved the way he did with him for a role model."

"So now what?" queried Paul. "How are you going to work with this father to help his son?"

"I can't work with that jerk," Tony exclaimed.

"That's not an option you have, Tony. You can't opt out of a relationship with the father of a student, even a difficult parent like this one."

Paul continued, "There's something else that's not computing for me here. I know you. I've watched you work with kids. You are a terrific teacher, and you really care about your students. I've seen you go to great extra lengths to help them succeed. I've also seen you handle really difficult parents very effectively. You're the one who's always reminding the mentorship group to be compassionate and hang in there in tough situations."

"So it seems out of character for you to be shouting back at an angry parent and claiming that you can't work with him because he's such a jerk. What's up with you?"

"You're right, Paul, this is not like me. I need to think about what's going on with me that I blew it like this."

Paul responded, "I think that's a good idea. You want to learn from this situation so you're less likely to do it again. Maybe it's time to add a few new skills about managing your reactivity with difficult people. If it's all right with you, I'd like to discuss this in our mentorship group tomorrow. Everyone of you will be faced with parents like this, so I think you could all benefit from this experience. As a group, we can help you consider what to do next with both the parent and his son."

"In the meantime, I want you to do some damage control, Tony. I suggest you give a heads up to the principal. That parent probably has him on speed dial. Let the principal know that we are working on a plan to rectify the situation."

Paul was able to stay spiritually present with Tony after Tony's verbal battle with the parent. Paul reminded Tony of what he had observed about him, which was inconsistent with his response to the parent. This dose of reality helped Tony to begin thinking more clearly about the situation. Now, Tony can find a way to respond differently to this parent and other challenging people in his workplace. In the long run, Paul will help Tony learn to remain spiritually present no matter what he is facing.

Each of us finds it easier to be present in some circumstances than in others and with some people rather than others. We may find one form of presence comes more easily to us than the others. With conscious effort, we can learn to be present in ways that seem less natural for us.

The goal is to become more balanced so that we are more able to be present in all four ways—physically, mentally, emotionally, and spiritually—in as many circumstances and with as many types of people as possible. The more balanced we are, the easier and more natural it will be for us to have successful difficult conversations. Balance is a life's work, not something we can acquire overnight. We achieve this balance through the choices we make each day. This is the path of the warrior/leader.

Pay Attention to What Has Heart and Meaning

The cross-cultural archetype of the healer asks that you pay attention to what has heart and meaning for you—not what your parents value, not what your spouse holds dear, not what your friends think you should do—what is important to *you*. What you value most fuels your passion for life and work. When you act from what has heart and meaning, you have integrity because you are fully aligned with your core self.

When you live from your values, it is easier to be open-hearted with others and to be fully enthusiastic about your work. It is also more comfortable to make decisions that serve you well and to say "no" when opportunities are not right for you. In addition, when you do not have clarity, it is easier for you to wait until the murk clears before you make a decision. When you are centered, you are more likely to find happiness and contentment with what is, rather than always wishing for what you don't have.

Dan loved teaching high school speech and debate. His passion was getting shy kids to express themselves. Dan's father was a principal in another school district, and he counseled Dan to go to graduate school to get his principal's license. Dan had great respect for his father, so he dutifully completed his master's in educational leadership and served an internship to get his license.

The next step was to apply for a job as an assistant principal. Dan found himself putting off filling out applications. He began to wonder if he was afraid of taking on the responsibilities that would come with being an administrator, but that didn't make sense. He had learned that he had some talent for leadership, and he did not mind the details that went with administration. So, what was the problem?

As Dan listened to himself carefully, he realized that what was missing was passion—he had no fire for being a principal. It didn't excite him. Dan finally realized that he was trying to live his father's dream, rather than his own. He recognized that his father had placed himself exactly where he belonged, in the principalship. Now, Dan understood that he also needed to take responsibility for himself. For Dan, this meant staying in the classroom, his own true home. With relief, he tore up the applications. Then, he sought out his dad for a heart-felt difficult conversation.

It was only when Dan was actually faced with leaving his classroom that he finally listened to his heart. Thankfully, he realized that the right placement for him meant staying put. How easy it is to think that moving into management will automatically provide greater happiness. If it is not where you belong, then it will not be satisfying.

There are also other consequences for not listening to your inner knowing. When you do not pay attention to what has heart and meaning for you, there is a greater likelihood that you will feel that you are being victimized. You are the only one who can give your life meaning. If you are not taking that responsibility, you are likely to get yourself into situations where you feel that you are at the mercy of others. If you are not the actor, you are the acted upon.

If you are not in touch with what is really important to you, it will be much more difficult for you to hold your own in a difficult conversation. You will be less able to state your point of view convincingly without shaming or blaming the other person. Speaking from your heart is the most compelling form of communication.

> Denise began teaching in the middle of a school year in a large, urban high school. It was the first year that black children were bussed into this previously all-white, blue-collar neighborhood.
>
> In one of her sophomore English classes, Denise had a student named Anthony, who slept through every class and never handed in any assignments. Anthony's best friend whispered to Denise that Anthony's father was drunk every night and that he was so violent that Anthony frequently stayed out all night to protect himself. He could never get enough rest in the park or on the floor of the laundromat. In those pre-child protection days, Denise decided to let Anthony sleep in her class, where he felt safe.
>
> In the spring, Martin Luther King, Jr. was assassinated. Denise, who had been inspired and called to action by Dr. King, mourned the loss of one of her personal heroes. Meanwhile, riots broke out a few miles from the high school. Helicopters flew overhead, and there were armed guards in the halls. The atmosphere in the school was tense, and many white parents kept their children at home.
>
> Denise was appalled when the administration did not lower the flag to half mast when Dr. King died and when they carried on school business as if there had not been a great loss. Because of her strong convictions, Denise decided that Steinbeck and Hemingway would have to wait,

and she opened up a discussion with her students about race.

Denise told her sophomore English class, with tears in her eyes, about the gift to her life that Dr. King and his teachings had been. Inspired by her openness and depth of feeling, the students talked freely for the first time about what it was like to be in a newly integrated school. Denise asked her students to write essays about their ideas for how black and white people could learn to live and work together in harmony. She offered a prize for the best essay.

Denise was surprised when she received a 30-page essay from Anthony. It was eloquent and well written and was the clear winner of the contest. When Anthony was called to the front of the class to receive his award, he merely took the pencil and pen set and nodded. Denise saw that Anthony had a gift for writing and hoped that he would continue to participate, but he went back to sleep. Denise carried her sorrow for Anthony when she moved to another state at the end of the school year.

Seven years later, Denise received a card in the mail. It was old-fashioned and yellow and looked like it had been in a grandmother's bureau drawer for twenty years. The handwritten message inside read, "I want you to know that what you said about Martin when he was killed meant a lot to me. Writing that essay changed my life. I graduated from college this week. Thank you, Anthony."

Although she did not know it at the time, Denise was finally able to reach Anthony when she spoke from her deepest feelings and convictions. Anthony had been in pain about the loss of Dr. King, and he was surprised and deeply touched when his white teacher expressed similar feelings. It was a healing experience for both Denise and Anthony. This is the way of the healer archetype.

Tell the Truth without Blame or Judgment

By paying attention to what has heart and meaning for you, you are in a position to say what is true for you. This is your truth, not the ultimate Truth. It is your view of the world from where you sit.

When you do not dare to say what is true for you, you are likely to do one of several unproductive things. You may try to keep the peace at any price by appeasing the other person. This is a form of denial. Or, taking appeasement to an extreme, you may suffer in silence, inflate the problem, and believe yourself to be a martyr. At the other extreme, you may act out your dissatisfaction or frustration. In this covert way, you may make indirect snide comments or resort to other passive aggressive behavior.

If something is bothering you, telling the truth means being straightforward and direct about it with the other person. You let that person know what her impact on you has been. You are specific, so that she will know exactly to which of her behaviors you are referring. Saying what is true for you has a cleansing effect. Being honest brings you into authenticity, and that feels good; however, frankness is not enough to help you connect with the other person. Recall the first story in Chapter One of this book, in which Estelle was always straightforward, but people rarely heard what she had to say because she was so scathing in her delivery.

It takes personal discipline to not indulge in shaming, blaming, or judging while you are saying what is true for you. In successful difficult conversations, there is not an attempt to punish or show up the other person. Instead of blaming each other, the parties work together to sort out their contributions to the situation. If you are blaming and judging, you are not working toward a win/win solution.

Carmen was the administrative assistant to Anne, her district's director of communications. Together, they published a monthly newsletter for all of the parents in the district. Anne gathered the articles, and then Carmen formatted, printed, and mailed the finished newsletter.

Carmen approached Anne for a difficult conversation: "Anne, I'm frustrated with you about the newsletter. You and I have an agreement that you will give me your copy by 8 a.m. the day before I publish the newsletter, but it isn't happening. For the past three months, you have given me your articles at the end of the day instead. That means that I have to stay here until midnight to get the newsletter out on time. You keep laughing and telling me that you are 'the queen of procrastination,' but it isn't funny. In the last three months, your procrastination has caused me to miss two of my son's hockey games and my daughter's dance recital. I value making the newsletter really good each month and getting it out on time. And, I'm not willing to continue to give up my evenings because you don't have your copy finished."

Anne replied, "I've really been oblivious to my impact on you. You do such a spectacular job on the newsletter; I never gave a thought about how you get it done. I just dump the work on you and make a joke about my procrastination and leave for home. I don't want you to have to spend another evening working on the newsletter. It's not okay if my procrastination affects you. I'm really sorry. You can count on me to meet my deadlines with you in the future."

Carmen was clear and provided specific examples of how Anne's procrastination had negatively affected her. Even though she was angry, Carmen did not allow herself to descend into being shaming. This tactic created an opening for Anne to take responsibility for her own behavior and to make amends. Anne also said what was true for herself without blame or judgment. This is the practice of the visionary archetype.

Be Open to Outcome, Not Attached to Outcome

When you have managed to be fully present, have rooted your self in your heart, and have said what is true for you without blame or judgment, the final step is to let go of the outcome. You only have control of what you say and do, not of how others receive your input. If you have been clean and clear in a difficult conversation, you can walk away from it feeling good about yourself, regardless of the outcome.

This principle also holds true when someone approaches you to complain. If you are able to remain present, stay centered, and be honest, you will be able to receive difficult feedback, change your behavior when necessary, and like yourself at the end of the process.

Tom decided to become a principal because he had a deep belief in justice, and he wanted all students to have a fair chance to learn. He was midway through his first year in a new principalship when three African-American teachers walked into his office. They had their arms crossed over their chests, and they looked at him through narrowed eyes. Rebecca spoke for the group: "It looks to us like you are disciplining black students far more harshly than you are white students. That's racism, Mr. Perkins, and we won't stand for it."

Tom's stomach turned over—the last thing he wanted to be was racist. He took a slow, deep breath and responded. "Thank you for coming to me directly with your concerns. I hope you're wrong. If you're right, and I am discriminating against anyone, I need to change my behavior. Here are all of the discipline slips for the year so far. Will you work with me to compile the data so that we can get an accurate picture of how I have been disciplining both black and white students?"

Tom and the three teachers compared the nature and severity of students' offenses with the level of discipline that Tom had meted out with the race and gender of the students. When all of the information was collated, it was clear that Tom had been even-handed as a disciplinarian. The teachers were relieved, a little embarrassed, and puzzled. Tom was just relieved.

In trying to sort out what had given them the impression that Tom was being unfair, the teachers realized that a disproportionate percentage of African-American students came to them to complain when they were disciplined. Tom realized that his discipline process lacked transparency and consequently was open to misinterpretation. He decided to publish discipline statistics quarterly so that teachers, students, and parents could see for themselves if punishment was being handled fairly. The teachers left with a new sense of trust in their principal.

Tom did not move into defensiveness when he was accused of being racist. He was able to do this because his work was grounded in his love of justice and because he was able to maintain his own sense of sufficiency. Even though the teachers were angry with him, he recognized that they wanted the same thing he wanted—equity for everyone. Tom was guided by his character, not his ego. All of this allowed Tom to be open to the possibility that he had acted in an unconsciously racist manner. He was willing to change his behavior if the data showed a need. He was open to outcome, not attached to outcome. The teachers were also willing to look again at Tom in light of new information. This journey of flexibility is the one suggested by the teacher archetype.

When you are attached to outcome, you have an agenda, and you will work it any way that you can. Rather than letting natural outcomes emerge, you will try to control people and circumstances to get your way. Even if your intentions are good, you may make a mess with the means you use to accomplish them. No one likes to be manipulated. Control is the opposite of trust and is the shadow side of the teacher archetype.

The ability to let go when things are over is another attribute of the teacher archetype. If you are open to outcome, you can accept the way things turn out, rather than hanging on and hoping for something different. It is important to have clear endings to chapters of your work life. At the end of a unit, a school year, a career, it is important to celebrate and move on with your life. One of the purposes of difficult conversations is to put closure to difficult chapters so that you do not have to carry problems around with you for weeks, months, or years. You will be most successful in having difficult conversations if you are able to be present, to pay attention to what has heart and meaning for you, to say what is true for you without blame or judgment, and to let go of the outcome.

Each of the four archetypes can serve as your ally in making your work and your life richly rewarding. The energy that you spend in employing the cross-cultural skills of the warrior/leader, the healer, the visionary, and the teacher will leave you feeling renewed and whole. It is a life's work to find a balance between all four archetypes.

Chapter Summary

The cross-cultural archetypes of the warrior/leader, healer, visionary, and teacher provide a structural overview for successful difficult conversations. The way of the warrior/leader is to show up and be present in four ways: physically, mentally, emotionally, and spiritually. Being fully present allows you to access and use your personal power in a responsible manner. The way of the healer is to pay attention to what has heart and meaning in order to be able to speak clearly about what is of value to you. The visionary's path is to tell the truth without blame or judgment so that others will be able to hear what you have to say. The task of the teacher is to be open to outcome, not attached to outcome, so that you can do your best and feel personally successful, no matter what the other person does. These are the elements of a successful difficult conversation.

CAUSES OF CONFLICT IN THE WORKPLACE

Chapter 3

The Roles of Task and Relationship in Workplace Conflict

Difficult conversations are required whenever there is conflict in the workplace. Successful difficult conversations require an understanding of what is causing the conflict. Every workplace conflict relates to problems in carrying out tasks, problems that colleagues have relating to each other, or some combination of the two. This chapter examines the role of task and relationship in workplace conflict.

Before we continue, please think about the way you deal with tasks and relationships in your workplace. Are you more likely to focus on getting things done or on building relationships with your colleagues? Give yourself a number on this continuum.

0	5	10
Task		Relationship

Make a note of the number you have assigned yourself, and we will come back to it later in the chapter.

33

Conflict is created when there is a vacuum, or lack of information, in either task or relationship. One set of problems is created when there is a vacuum of data related to tasks, and a different set of problems is created when there is a vacuum related to relationships.

Vacuums Related to Tasks

Educators must accomplish many tasks every day. Sometimes the sheer number of things that need to be done can feel overwhelming. Lack of clarity about how things are to be accomplished creates unnecessary stress and can also lead to conflict, which can only be resolved through difficult conversations.

Everyone involved in accomplishing a task or a set of tasks needs to have the same information. Here are some of the elements of information about tasks that can cause problems if they are missing.

What and How?

It is important to have agreement about what the task is. What are we trying to accomplish?

> Patricia and Carlos were responsible for scheduling all of the freshman and sophomores for the coming high school year. They decided that they would each schedule one of the grades. When they had finished, they came back together with their results. To their dismay, they discovered that they had both been scheduling students into some of the same classes and lunch periods. As a result, some classes had been assigned more than seventy students, and the lunch periods were unworkably imbalanced in numbers. The scheduling mess was further compounded when Patricia and Carlos discovered that there was also unforeseen overlap with the junior and senior schedules. Several days' worth of work had to be redone. Both Patricia and Carlos felt frustrated and dreaded redoing the tedious job of scheduling.

Patricia and Carlos did not construct a clear map of the task that they were to accomplish or anticipate possible problems and how to resolve them. Consequently, they made unnecessary mistakes and created stress for themselves and the schedulers for the other grades. In order to fill this vacuum of information about what is to be accomplished, Patricia and Carlos will have to have a conversation that includes all of the schedulers so that they can determine what needs to be done and how to achieve it. They will need to construct a plan for dealing with classes that have students from multiple grade levels and for apportioning students to lunch periods. Their plan will need to be detailed and specific in order to succeed on the second try.

Why?

When the reasons for doing a task are not clear, confusion and conflict can result.

Ted and his student teacher, Eric, had just finished a basketball unit with their seventh graders. Ted asked Eric to pack up the basketball equipment and left for the day. Eric had worked with Ted to set up the unit, so he reversed the process in packing up. Eric got out the ladder and removed the extra backboards and hoops and carefully packed them with all the balls. Then, he took them to the corner of the school basement where they had been stored.

The next morning, Ted asked Eric, "What have you done with all of the basketball stuff?" Eric replied, "I did as you asked and packed it all up and put it back in the basement." Ted was angry, "You did what? I need all that equipment for the basketball team tryouts after school today. I wanted you to pack everything in the team bags! We need all the backboards for practice. You knew tryouts were today—what were you thinking?" Eric said, "I assumed the team had its own equipment." To which Ted replied, "Well, you assumed wrong! Go get all of it from the basement and start putting it back up. I don't know how you're going to manage with the ladder while the classes are playing dodge ball. I guess you'll just have to miss lunch." Now, Eric was angry, too.

Ted did not tell Eric why he was putting away the basketball equipment—that he was switching from class unit to school team storage. Ted needed to say clearly to Eric, "The basketball team will need all of this equipment tomorrow. Would you please pack the basketball equipment into these team bags. That will give us room to store the equipment for the next unit. You can leave the extra backboards where they are."

Eric compounded the problem by assuming that the team used different equipment and by not checking this conclusion with Ted. In the absence of sufficient information, Eric assumed he was to follow the same procedure that Ted had showed him in readying the equipment for the unit. As a result, they now need to have a difficult conversation about what went wrong in their communication so that they do not repeat this process again.

Who?

When there is a complex set of tasks to be performed, it is essential to be clear about who is responsible for which tasks.

An elementary school staff decided to have a picnic to kick off the school year. All of the teachers were to travel to a remote park for softball and a potluck. Tiffany, a teacher, was drafted to organize the event. She rented a pavilion with a ball field, organized carpooling to the event, and assigned people food items to bring. Tiffany talked the plans over with another teacher, Jennifer, and asked her to "pick up the supplies for the party."

When everyone reached the park, they laid out a feast of brats, potato salad, baked beans, chips, and pie. Tiffany told Jennifer it was time to set out the supplies. Jennifer went to her car and returned with bats, bases, gloves, and softballs. Tiffany said, "Where are the plates and napkins and utensils that I asked you to bring?" Jennifer replied, "I didn't know you wanted me to bring those things. I thought you were bringing them." Tiffany laughed ruefully and said, "Well, I brought softball equipment, too. We can have two softball games, but we're going to have to eat with our hands." They used the brats to shovel beans and potato salad onto their buns and scooped up pie with their chips. It was a picnic the staff never forgot.

Tiffany planned carefully for many of the details of the picnic. Things fell apart when she and Jennifer were not specific enough with each other about who was responsible for bringing which items to the party. Tiffany needed to say to Jennifer, "Will you pick up the plates, napkins, and plastic utensils for the whole group? You will be reimbursed out of petty cash." Alternatively, Jennifer could have said, "I just want to be clear. Are you asking me to bring the equipment for the softball game?"

This incident was humorous, and the staff was good natured about improvising. Imagine how differently this might have turned out if Tiffany and Jennifer had been planning a field trip for students to canoe through a marshland. If one had been responsible for bringing the paddles and the other the life jackets, the trip would have been ruined if they had ended up with either all paddles or all life jackets.

When?

Timeliness can be everything in accomplishing tasks.

Dick, a superintendent, was preparing for a school board meeting. The day before the meeting, he gave his secretary, Sally, a document to reproduce for the board, saying, "This is for the next board meeting."

At the meeting the following night, Dick reached into his folder for the copies of the document and found that they were not there. The document was Dick's proposal to the board for how to approach the upcoming public referendum for funding for the district. Dick was embarrassed that he did not have copies to give to the board.

The next morning, he confronted Sally, "I looked unprofessional last night because you didn't make the copies that I requested." Sally, looking startled, replied, "But you said they were for the next meeting." "Oh," groaned Dick, "You thought I meant the meeting two weeks from now." Sally nodded. Dick said, "I apologize for being unclear and for taking it out on you. I'll try to be more specific in the future." Sally smiled and responded, "Thanks, Dick. I know you're human. How about sending them each a copy of your proposal today?" It was Dick's turn to nod.

Dick learned an important lesson about the need to be specific about any deadlines for work that he gave Sally. He also understood that he needed to be careful not to blame someone else when he felt embarrassed professionally.

How Do You Know When You've Been Successful?

When the standards for success of a project are clearly defined, you know when you are finished, when you have done a good job, and when it's time to celebrate. Without clear criteria for success, the task may seem never ending, and you may not agree on when you have accomplished your goals.

Derrick, the principal of an inner-city high school, was approached by a council of local small-business owners who were concerned about the damage caused to their establishments by truant students. Derrick told the council members that he and his administrators were concerned about the truancy problem, too, and were about to launch an effort to reduce the occurrence of students skipping school. He asked the council to give them six months to change the situation. They agreed.

Derrick and his staff introduced several innovative programs to keep students in school: mentorship programs, school-workplace partnerships, high school students tutoring elementary students, and academic units focused on urban culture. In six months, they reduced the truancy rate in their school by 60%.

Pleased and satisfied, Derrick invited the business owners back to his school. As they entered his office, he was surprised and puzzled when he saw that their faces were sullen and angry. The chairman of the council laid it out, "We gave you six months, and we have seen no change. We are still plagued by graffiti, shoplifting, and all manner of vandalism. What kind of school are you running here that teenagers can get away with this kind of trouble making?"

It was only then that Derrick realized that he and the council had different standards for measuring success. The school administrators felt successful because they had so greatly reduced the occurrence of truancy. The business owners were measuring success by the number of headaches and amount of financial losses caused by problem teenagers. Creating a successful solution for the council would apparently require a different set of strategies on the part of the school.

Derrick and his staff did great work with their students and were right in feeling proud and successful about lowering the truancy rate so dramatically. Where Derrick failed was in working to get a common agreement with the council on how to measure the success of the project from the business owners' point of view. He needed to find out what it would take to make them satisfied. In fact, they may actually have been trying to solve two different problems. This oversight cost Derrick credibility in the community.

Consequences of Vacuums Related to Tasks

As we have seen, the components of tasks are who, what, when, why, and how, combined with clear criteria for success. When these elements are sufficiently accounted for, things run smoothly, and the troops are happier. When there are vacuums related to tasks, a host of problems can lead to organizational breakdown and dissent.

When there is missing information about tasks, genuine disagreements may not emerge until too late in the process. We may think we are all on the same page when actually we don't agree on what we are doing and why. We may have very different assumptions about what a successful outcome should look like. If our differences were clear from the beginning, we could have an opportunity to negotiate through them before the situation became highly charged.

Without clear agreements about tasks, time and energy are wasted. Some vacuums around tasks keep work from being completed on time or sabotage projects from being completed at all. It is difficult to hold people accountable if it is not clear who is responsible for what. The people who are trying to do the work become frustrated and may turn on each other in anger. Workers trust each other less at the end of the process, making the next task even more difficult to accomplish.

Beyond the immediate work group, when tasks become messy, other people in the organization are less willing to be supportive because it is not clear what they are being asked to support and why. Negative assumptions may be made about the competence and professionalism of those attempting to accomplish the task. Looking in from the outside, community members may lose faith in the organization.

Task Vacuums: The Solution

When there are tasks to be accomplished by two or more people, make sure that the answers to the questions listed below are overtly clear and agreed upon by all of the parties at the beginning of the project.

- Exactly what are we going to accomplish, in detail?
- Why are we doing this?
- How do we propose to make it happen, specifically?
- Who is going to do each task?
- What is the timeline for each task?
- Specifically, how will we know when we are successful?

For complex tasks, it helps to write down the answers to the questions and give them to each member of the work group. For long-range projects, it is useful to check in with each other periodically to report progress, ask for help with snags, cheer each other on, and renegotiate the details, if necessary.

In each of the examples above, unchecked assumptions played a role in creating problems. In every instance, both of the participants made assumptions and did not ask the other person if they were accurate. Patricia and Carlos each assumed that the other person was doing scheduling each other's way. Ted assumed that Eric knew that the basketball team used the same equipment they had used in class. Eric made the opposite assumption. Tiffany and Jennifer each assumed that the other was bringing plates, napkins, and plastic utensils to the picnic. Dick assumed that Sally knew he was talking about the meeting the next day, and Sally assumed that Dick meant the meeting in two weeks. Derrick assumed that the business council wanted to reduce truancy, when what they really wanted was to reduce vandalism and theft from their businesses. Acting on each one of these unchecked assumptions had a negative consequence, some more serious than others.

These examples illustrate two important principles in preventing problems involving tasks. First, both parties help to create each of these problems. In most conflictual situations, the participants bear equal responsibility for the mess, and it is important for both to examine their own contributions to the problem. Owning your own part helps to prevent blaming the other person. Second, a cardinal rule of eliminating vacuums related to task is to check all assumptions by asking the other person directly about them.

Vacuums Related to Relationships

At least eighty percent of conflicts in the workplace result from vacuums related to relationships. In part, this is because many professionals tend to focus on the tasks that they have to accomplish and believe that they have no time to devote to tending to their work relationships. This is a shortsighted view of priorities. The accomplishment of tasks is essential, but it is not sufficient to make an organization run smoothly.

Problems related to tasks are usually more straightforward and more easily resolved than problems related to relationships. When things get heated between work colleagues, there is always a relationship issue to be resolved. Taking the time to maintain relationships is far more cost effective than wasting the time and energy required to unscramble relationship problems.

At work, we want to know that we matter and that we can make a difference. We want to know that we are liked as colleagues and that our work is respected. We want to be able to make meaning out of the actions and attitudes of others toward us. We want to know that we are being treated fairly and the same as other employees are being treated. These elements are the stuff of relationships in the workplace. When we do not know all of these things, we experience vacuums of relationship. Being human, when we don't have this information, we tend to make it up. We assign meaning where it is missing and often jump to the worst possible conclusion. Usually, we are wrong.

Let's look at the categories of missing information that can lead to vacuums related to relationship. These categories are questions about where we stand with other people in the workplace.

Can I Make Any Difference with You?

When you do not feel listened to or responded to, you tend to believe that you can have no impact on the other person. Similarly, if you believe that the person has already made up his mind about you and nothing you do will convince him otherwise, you may feel invisible. In any of these instances, it will be very difficult for you to figure out where you stand with the other person.

> Tyler was a high school English teacher and the boys' varsity soccer coach. He asked to meet with Brad, his athletic director, to present his ideas about how to schedule the use of the soccer field more effectively. When Tyler arrived in Brad's office, Brad offered him a seat and said, "Yes?" While Tyler presented his ideas, Brad sat with his feet up on the desk, tossing a baseball from hand to hand, looking out the window. Tyler found it difficult to stay focused and wondered if Brad was listening to him. When Tyler stopped speaking, Brad said, sarcastically, "Anything else, Dr. Sullivan? No? Shut the door on your way out." Tyler left silently

As he left Brad's office, Tyler was feeling frustrated and hopeless about his working relationship with Brad. This was not the first time that Brad had referred derogatorily to his Ph.D. He wanted Brad to be able to hear his ideas and to see him as a person, not a degree. He assumed this was impossible.

Brad made no attempt in this conversation to create a connection with Tyler. He did not inquire about how Tyler's team was doing or express any interest in Tyler as a person or a professional. Through his nonverbal language—putting his feet on the desk, tossing a baseball, and looking out the window—Brad appeared to be disinterested in Tyler's ideas. Brad also made a personal dig referring to Brad's advanced degree. Brad's role in the relationship vacuum is clear. What's not so obvious is that Tyler also played a part in creating the relationship vacuum.

Tyler had a high level of respect for Brad's abilities as an athletic director, but he had never let Brad know how he felt. Instead, Tyler just presented his ideas for change to Brad, who misinterpreted Tyler's intentions. Brad thought Tyler looked down on him and wanted his job. Tyler had never told Brad that he wanted to be a college English professor and soccer coach. Brad thought Tyler was the best soccer coach he had ever seen, but did not even let Tyler know that he thought he was doing a good job.

These men need to have a difficult conversation. Essentially, they need to start over with each other. Tyler needs to show the respect he feels for Brad and let him know he is not making negative assumptions about Brad when he offers ideas. Brad needs to take Tyler out of the "Dr. Know-It-All" pigeonhole that he has put him in and acknowledge Tyler's skill. These actions will fill the relationship vacuum between the two men and will allow them to work together on tasks much more effectively. Brad can then listen to Tyler's ideas and evaluate them without prejudice.

Do You Like Me?

Most of us want to be personally accepted by the people with whom we spend 40 hours a week. Personal regard helps us to feel accepted and included. When we are uncertain about whether someone likes us, we begin to speculate, and usually our assumptions are negative.

Pam taught seventh grade science. She was delighted when Amy joined the staff as a first year language arts teacher. They were about the same age, seemed to have similar interests, and tended to laugh at the same things. Pam loved to process her day by talking with a friend, and she invited Amy to go for a walk with her after school. The two talked for several hours about their students and their personal lives. Pam thought that she had a new friend, and she invited Amy to go for another walk. Amy politely declined. After several more attempts to get Amy to walk with her after school, Pam gave up. She was disappointed and troubled because they seemed to have hit it off so well in the beginning. Pam reached the conclusion that the relationship had been one-sided and that Amy didn't like her.

Pam didn't have to encounter Amy at school on a daily basis—their classrooms were in different wings of the building, and they had different prep and lunch periods. So Pam tried to ignore the situation, and she succeeded until she and Amy were assigned to the same curriculum committee. Pam decided that she needed to have a difficult conversation with Amy if they were going to work together.

Pam caught Amy in the parking lot after school. She said to Amy, "I want to check something out with you. I thought we had such a good time the one time we took a walk. When you didn't want to do it again, I assumed that you just didn't like me. Now that we're going to be on the curriculum committee together, I'd like to straighten this out. Am I right that you don't like me?"

Amy responded with tears in her eyes, "I'm so sorry, Pam. I did have a great time with you on that walk. I also paid for it the next day. I'm a real introvert—I need lots of alone time to regenerate. I had no idea how much energy it would take for me to be with seventh graders all day every day. I'm finding that I need to rush home and be alone and completely quiet so that there is enough of me to come back here the next day. That's why I have turned you down to go for another walk. I'm so sorry that you thought that I didn't like you. In fact, I was just about to ask you if you wanted to walk around the lake this Saturday."

Pam said, "I'm just the opposite—a real extrovert. I need to talk to another adult every day in order to keep myself fresh! No wonder I couldn't see why you didn't want to spend hours talking. I'd love to walk around the lake with you on Saturday."

In the absence of information about why Amy repeatedly turned her down to go walking, Pam assumed that Amy did not like her. By not providing Pam with a context for her refusals, Amy created a relationship vacuum. It was respectful of Pam to ask Amy for the missing information. Pam would have decreased her own stress level if she had asked sooner. If Amy and Pam are going to be good colleagues and possibly friends, they will have to honor and respect both Amy's introversion and Pam's extroversion.

The most vital organizations have a high tolerance for individual differences. There is room for the introverts and the extroverts, the night owls and the morning people, those who want to consider all of the options and those who want to make decisions quickly, those who react from their feelings and those who need to think things over, those who want to race through tasks and those who love to approach life at a stroll. No one is viewed as right or wrong, just different. This acceptance of differences creates an opportunity to utilize all of the skills of all of the players, not just those whose proclivities are popular.

Do You Respect My Work?

In addition to feeling personally valued, we also want to know that our work is respected. We want to know that our efforts are deemed to be worthwhile by others. We want to be viewed as professionally competent, and we want to know that our work is a vital part of the organizational whole. We particularly want to know that those in authority value our work.

Sean was a social worker who served three elementary schools. He had developed particular expertise in problems faced by adopted children. He volunteered to provide professional development training on this topic for all of the district's counselors, social workers, and psychologists. Sean worked hard for several months to prepare for this training, and his heart was beating fast as he stood in front of colleagues.

As he was speaking, Sean's attention returned repeatedly to Marie, the Assistant Superintendent for Student Services, who was his supervisor. Sean had a deep respect for Marie, both because of her wisdom and her position. Her opinion mattered more to him than anyone else's. Marie was sitting with her arms tightly crossed and had a sour expression on her face. Periodically, she grimaced and looked away. Sean thought, "She hates it. Maybe my presentation isn't as good as I thought. I must be blowing it."

After Sean's presentation, his colleagues surrounded him and told him how much they appreciated his material and how useful it would be in their work. Out of the corner of his eye, Sean could see Marie, holding back from the crowd and looking disgruntled.

Marie waited until everyone else had left the room and closed the door. Sean had a deepening feeling of dread about the feedback she would give him. Marie said, "I was so deeply moved by your presentation that I was afraid I was going to sob. I knew if I started, I wouldn't be able to stop." She continued with tears streaming down her face, " I was adopted, and when I was in school there was no help for what I was going through inside. I'm so deeply grateful that you are doing this work and that you made such a magnificent presentation to the staff. Thank you!"

It's sobering to think how easily we can jump to negative conclusions with very little information. Marie modeled self-responsibility in explaining herself as quickly as possible to Sean. Had she not done so, she would have created a relationship vacuum. Then it would have been Sean's responsibility to ask her for feedback in order to set his fears to rest.

We have seen that nonverbal language, facial expressions, and lack of context can lead to misunderstandings that create relationship vacuums. There are also many other elements to communication that can be similarly misinterpreted. We may wonder what a person's tone of voice means. Is he angry? What about? At me? We may suspect the timing in which something occurs. Did she bring that up now to make me look bad in front of our colleagues?

Are You Discriminating against Me?

Take any of the examples above and insert a major difference between the two people. What if Tyler, the soccer coach, had been a Muslim who thought Brad, his Baptist athletic director, would not listen to him because of their religious differences? What if Pam had believed that Amy didn't want to walk with her anymore because she had discovered that Pam was a lesbian? What if Sean had been African American and assumed that Marie, his white supervisor, didn't think he could do high-level professional work because he was black?

It is very difficult for anyone in a minority group to know how to interpret a relationship vacuum. There is always the possibility that the cause could be discrimination or prejudice. One of the best ways of welcoming diversity in the workplace is to prevent vacuums of relationship from occurring and to fill the voids as quickly as possible when they do occur. The discipline of the minority person is to treat the assumption of discrimination like any other assumption and not act on it without asking for more information.

Relationship Vacuums: The Solution

We need to give the people we work with enough information so that they know where they stand with us. When we are missing information about others, we need to ask for it. Here are specific ways to prevent relationship vacuums from forming and to fill them once they have happened.

♦ Listen to your colleagues. Ask clarifying questions to make sure you understand what they are saying.

Seek to understand what is important to them and why.

- Make yourself visible to your colleagues by letting them know what you value and where you stand on key issues. Don't put your work mates in a position of guessing what you think or of dragging your opinions out of you.

- Take ten seconds to acknowledge the importance of your work relationships in most interactions. Showing that you care can be as simple as a hand on a shoulder, a smile, or saying "thank you." Use your sense of humor to connect with your colleagues.

- Give your colleagues feedback about the impact of their behavior on you. Let them know when you feel supported, inspired, and tickled by them. Also let them know when you feel mistreated, insulted, or taken for granted. Accurate feedback, without blame or judgment, is one of the greatest gifts that you can give to a colleague.

- Welcome and solicit feedback from your colleagues about your impact on them. Develop your ability to receive and incorporate difficult information about yourself. Without a feedback loop, it is easy to have an impact that you do not intend. Take responsibility for your impact. Apologize. Take corrective action. Show by your altered behavior that your impact on others matters to you. Changing your behavior is a way of showing respect for your colleagues and yourself.

- When you don't understand a colleague's facial expression, tone of voice, or intentions, ask. Pose the question within one week to get the most meaningful response. On the spot is even better. Timeliness will also keep you from creating more stress for yourself by waiting to speak. Resist the urge to get creative with your interpretations of others' actions. Mind reading is disrespectful and leads to conflict.

♦ Be yourself. Don't try to guess what others want you to be and then try to deliver it. Speak from your heart. Dare to make mistakes. Take responsibility for mistakes when you make them. Connection is a messy human process.

Vacuums related to relationships touch the core of our human needs to be accepted and appreciated and to make a difference in the world. In the workplace, we have dual responsibilities when it comes to relationships. We need to make our own intentions, feelings, and thoughts toward others clear. On the other hand, when we do not perceive that clarity in others' actions toward us, we need to ask for the missing information. As we have seen with vacuums related to tasks, vacuums related to relationships are co-created.

The Interactions of Vacuums Related to Tasks and Vacuums Related to Relationships

It is useful to think of tasks as the bones of the organization and relationships as the connective tissue. Relationships are what animate tasks and bring them alive. The body of the organization will not work with either all bones or all connective tissue. It requires both tasks and relationships to function. If the organization is overfocused on tasks, people feel taken for granted and underappreciated. Burnout is more likely. Conversely, if there is an overemphasis on relationships, the work of the organization does not get accomplished. A balance of task and relationship creates both optimal work success and highly satisfied employees.

When there is a vacuum related to task, eventually it will also result in a vacuum related to relationship. Vacuums related to relationship also may prevent people from accomplishing important work tasks together.

Rebecca was the principal of the district kindergarten center. She had a leadership team comprised of three teachers, one specialist, a paraprofessional, her assistant, and herself. Rebecca was a hard worker and expected her leadership team to work hard, too. She gave specific assignments with deadlines to each team member. The weekly team meetings were very focused, and the group accomplished many tasks.

All of the team members felt honored when Rebecca asked them to participate. For a while, everything on the team worked smoothly. Then Rebecca noticed that everyone but her assistant was beginning to look a bit sullen in the meetings, which seemed flat. Before long, some of the members were not accomplishing the tasks assigned to them. Rebecca wondered if she had picked the right people for the team.

When team members started to make barbed, indirect comments in the meetings, Rebecca realized that she needed to take action. She asked the team for feedback about what it was like for them to work together. Their comments surprised Rebecca. "Do you think we're just machines?" "We've been doing great work, and you have never given us any positive feedback." "I feel taken for granted." "I want to have some fun while we work."

Rebecca realized that she had imposed her own nose-to-the-grindstone style on the team. She confessed to the members, "I do appreciate your work. You have been fabulous! Together, we have made this an excellent kindergarten center. I don't pat myself on the back, so I don't think to do it to others. It doesn't mean that I don't value you. You have my commitment that I will work to give you regular feedback and appreciation, rather than just keeping it to myself. I'm willing to try to make the meetings more enjoyable, but it's not my strong suit. What ideas do you have to make our work more fun?"

Rebecca had become too focused on accomplishing tasks and had neglected her relationships with her leadership team members. This imbalance eventually led to the members' being unwilling to work on tasks. The members' part in this problem was that they did not proactively ask for what they wanted.

Instead, they acted out their feelings by becoming sullen, stopping work, and making inappropriate comments.

Rebecca corrected the situation when she initiated a difficult conversation with the team and took their comments about the impact of her behavior on their morale seriously. The long-term effectiveness of the leadership team will depend on Rebecca's ability to keep a balance between task and relationship and on the members' willingness to speak up when they don't like what's happening.

Personal Orientation toward Either Task or Relationship

Rebecca's story is not unusual. Many of us have an imbalance in our orientation toward either task or relationship. If Rebecca had been highly oriented toward relationship, she might have made the opposite mistake with her team by spending too much time on building connection and appreciating the team members. Then they would have been clamoring, "Can we just get the job done!" A balance between task and relationship is needed. Sometimes our own tendencies get in the way of accomplishing this balance.

Recall the continuum from task to relationship on which you ranked yourself at the beginning of the chapter.

0	5	10
Task		Relationship

Through a combination of nature and nurture, each of us has a place on that continuum where we currently feel most comfortable at work. Anyone with a ranking of 0, 1, or 2 is *highly task oriented*. Those with rankings of 8, 9, or 10 are *highly relationally oriented*. There are strengths in both ends of the spectrum, and they are most powerful when there is a balance of both sets of skills. The good news is that you can learn to achieve more of a balance between task and relationship in your work life.

Both high taskers and high relaters care about the work and the people involved, but they express their caring in very different ways. When these differences are not understood, they can lead to conflict in the workplace. Let's look at the style differences between high taskers and high relaters in detail.

What Is Most Important to You?

Both high-task educators and high-relationship educators care deeply about the well-being of children and helping them to learn. The way they express their caring may be very different. High taskers tend to be passionate about curriculum, classroom structure, and classroom management. On the other hand, high relaters tend to be passionate about people and how they are treated, meaning, and tradition. Those in the middle of the spectrum (3, 4, 5, 6, or 7 on the continuum) tend to use a blend of these two strategies.

♦ Gregory, who ranked himself as a 1 on the task-relationship continuum, used rules and structure to maintain order with his fifth grade students. Although his classroom was often quiet, some students chafed under Gregory's regimen, and he frequently sent students to the principal for further discipline. Some parents thought Gregory was too harsh and seemed uncaring about individual children.

♦ Steve ranked himself at the opposite of the spectrum with a 9 on the continuum. He used hugs, teasing, and special privileges to influence his students. The fifth graders loved Steve and said they enjoyed being in his class. However, other teachers sometimes complained about the noise his students created, and some parents were concerned that their children were not learning enough in Steve's class.

♦ Randall, a self-described 5 on the task-relationship continuum, used a blend of Gregory's and Steve's styles in working with his fifth grade class. Randall used structure to create a safe and harmonious work environment for his students, and he worked to maintain a strong connection with each individual boy and girl. Students liked his class, and parents were pleased with the academic progress of their children.

In order to be as effective as they want to be as teachers, both Gregory and Steve need to learn to utilize the skill set at the opposite end of the task-relationship continuum. Gregory needs to lighten up a bit and make more warm connections with each of his students. Steven needs to tighten up by creating more structure and order.

How Do You Include Others and Approach Problems?

High taskers attempt to include others by making them part of tasks. High relaters attempt to include others by telling them how they feel.

Similarly, those who are highly task oriented tend to find solutions for problems by taking action and creating policies, procedure, and rules. On the other hand, those who are highly relationally oriented may want to complain about problems in order to be heard and validated, not necessarily to attempt to resolve the problem.

High taskers tend to feel included when they have roles in important tasks. High relaters tend to feel included when they feel listened to and valued for themselves.

Gretchen, an eighth grade language arts teacher, dropped into her principal Allison's office after school and plopped into a chair. "After the fire drill this morning, I couldn't get the class to settle down. Janet D. put five pieces of bubble gum in her mouth while we were outside and blew the biggest bubble I have ever seen. The wind came up, and it popped and covered her face and half her head. Her eyebrows and hair were matted with gum. I had to send to the cafeteria for ice to harden up the gum. The kids thought it was hysterical, and I couldn't get them to calm down. I'm so discouraged because this was the day I was going to start my short story unit. I've worked so hard on it, and getting them excited from the beginning is the key to the success of the whole project. I don't want to see another piece of bubble gum in my life!"

Allison's response was, "I'm frustrated about gum, too. I've been noticing more and more wads of gum around the building. It's under the table in the cafeteria and stuck to the floor in the gym. When our track team was on TV last week, half the students were chewing gum. It looked awful! Gretchen, you understand the gum problem. Will you chair a faculty committee to come up with a policy about gum in the building?"

Gretchen said reluctantly, "Well, I guess I could do that," and she got up and left the office. Allison thought, "That was satisfying. I responded to Gretchen and began the process of finding a solution to the gum problem." Gretchen thought, "Allison—what a jerk! All I wanted was a little sympathy about my day, and I didn't get it. Instead, I have to chair this stupid gum committee."

Gretchen and Allison had a missed communication because of their difference in styles. Gretchen, a high relater, wanted to tell her principal about her bad day so that she could get sympathy and reassurance from Allison.

The response she wanted from Allison was something like, "Oh, Gretchen, how disappointing to have the fire drill and the gum mess happen on the first day of your new unit. I know how hard you've worked on this unit and what a creative beginning you have planned." It would also have helped if Allison had helped Gretchen to see the humor in the situation.

Allison felt sympathetic with Gretchen. Being a high tasker, she tried to be responsive to Gretchen by looking for a solution to the problem and giving Gretchen an important role as committee chair. Allison walked away believing this was a successful interaction. Gretchen left feeling that she had not been heard or cared about by Allison.

If Gretchen had understood their style differences, she could have started the conversation with Allison by saying, "I've had a bad day, and I just want a sympathetic ear. You don't need to do anything except listen to me and give me some encouragement."

This would signal Allison that Gretchen wanted to have a relational conversation, rather than a task conversation.

Alternatively, when Allison moved into problem-solving mode, Gretchen could have said, "Hey, I just want you to listen to my bad day and show some caring. In my mind, this is not a problem to be solved." Certainly, Gretchen should not have agreed to chair the committee when she did not want to do it.

On her end, Allison could have asked Gretchen, "Do you want me to do anything about this or are you looking for a sympathetic ear?" It's a great question for a high tasker. Often, people only want to be heard, and, if we rush off to try to fix something in response, the result will produce misunderstanding and conflict. Allison could still have addressed the gum problem at a different time and in a different way.

What Is Your Response to Rules, Procedures, and Assignments?

People who are highly task oriented tend to be comfortable making and following rules that support the accomplishment of tasks. On the other hand, high relaters view extensive rules and procedures as negative assumptions about their professional competence and good sense.

High taskers tend to feel undervalued when their work on tasks is not appreciated. Conversely, the more additional tasks high relaters are given, the more undervalued they feel.

High taskers feel frustrated by things that they view as hindrances to accomplishing important tasks. On the other hand, high relaters feel frustrated when tasks seem to be more important than people.

Keisha was the principal of a high school, and Bradley was her assistant principal. With budget cuts, they had lost their cafeteria supervisors and needed to ask teachers to rotate through cafeteria duty. This meant shortened lunch periods for the teachers with no additional pay.

Keisha's impulse was to be very matter of fact about the situation and send the teachers an e-mail with the new lunch duty schedule. Bradley cautioned, "There are going to be lots of strong feelings about this. I suggest that we lay out the problem for the teachers at a meeting and ask for their help. We need to let them know this was a last resort for us, and we care that it will have an impact that they don't like. We need the support of both the high taskers and the high relaters."

Keisha agreed to Bradley's plan. She was a high tasker and recognized that she tended to pursue tasks in a way that sometimes alienated the high relaters on her staff. She had hired Bradley, a high relater, to provide her with a more balanced perspective.

Keisha's original idea of conveying the information about lunch duty in an e-mail may have been enough for high-task teachers, provided they believed in the task. It would not have satisfied the high relaters. Keisha was astute in hiring an assistant who could provide the perspective of high relaters, which she struggled to see. As she works with Bradley, Keisha will need to acquire some of his relational skills, and he will need to learn more about tasks from her. In future roles, they may not have someone else to provide the balance for them, so each will need to be able to do it for him- or herself.

How Do You Respond to Change?

Highly task-oriented people tend to embrace change initiatives readily, and some even thrive on it. Highly relationally oriented people tend to be leery of changes that they feel may threaten people about whom they care deeply.

Not surprisingly, high taskers favor leaders who are change agents and will deal in facts and make sure that important tasks are accomplished. Conversely, high relaters like leaders who embrace tradition and are highly supportive of the status quo.

The school board hired Gene to be superintendent because he was dynamic and a progressive change agent. His charge was to "bring the school district into the twenty-first century by instituting current best practices."

Gene wanted everyone in the district to feel as if they owned the process of change, so he called for volunteers to be on a district-wide committee to study best practices and recommend changes. The group worked for a year and was proud of their final report with their detailed recommendations for change.

Gene and the committee were surprised when a sizeable portion of the district was adamantly opposed to the plan. "You're destroying everything we have worked so hard to create." "Lots of people will have to transfer to different buildings where they may not feel welcome." "We're real people, not just statistics on a page!"

Too late, Gene realized that the people who had volunteered were mostly highly task oriented. Their report did not address the concerns of the highly relationally oriented because they had not been represented on the committee. Gene thought that the requests of the high relaters could be addressed, but to do so now would not be as effective because the changes would come as an afterthought. It would take many difficult conversations to obtain a desirable result.

In any change initiative, the greatest feat is to recruit the whole organization in support of the effort. It is essential to seek out high relaters to be on the steering committee because they are not as likely to volunteer. Make it clear that the people are just as important as the task or the process.

The key to success with task and relationship is in obtaining a balance between the two. Clarity of task helps you to accomplish important work. Solid working relationships make it possible to maintain mutual respect, even when weathering difficult situations. It is not possible to keep task and relationship in harmonious balance without having difficult conversations.

Chapter Summary

Missing information in the workplace about either tasks or relationships can lead to conflict and become the subject of difficult conversations. In order to accomplish tasks effectively, it is important that everyone involved has the following information:

the reason for the task, how and when it will be accomplished, who will do each part of the work, the deadlines, and how success will be determined.

Workplace relationships must be strong enough to allow for disagreement and clear enough to be able to resolve conflict. This does not mean that you have to like each other. On the job, each person needs to know that he or she can make a difference, be heard, be valued as a contributor, and be respected. Absent this information, people tend to make negative assumptions about where they stand with others.

Each person has an orientation about how he or she attends to task and relationship in the workplace. On a continuum of task to relationship, those who are highly task oriented may see the world quite differently from those who are highly relationally oriented. These two groups may disagree on what is most important to them; how they view rules, procedures, and assignments; how they respond to change; and what makes them feel valued and frustrated. Neither approach is right: they are just different. Through difficult conversations, high taskers and high relaters can understand and respect each other's point of view and avoid misunderstanding and conflict.

Chapter 4

Villain, Victim, and Rescuer at Work

In the workplace, there are three roles that are always destructive: the villain, the victim, and the rescuer. You will play each of these roles at some time in your career. The behaviors associated with all three roles are never constructive and are often destructive, to you personally and to the work you share with others. It is important to remember that these are assumed roles, not who you really are. You are always free to choose to shed the role and opt for more constructive interactions.

The behaviors associated with all three of these roles lead to conflict on the job. They also make success in difficult conversations less easy, if not impossible, to achieve. Any time you are playing a role, rather than being yourself, you will not be reliable in difficult conversations. An understanding of each of the roles helps you stay out of them. It takes all three roles to construct an unproductive triangle. The next chapter addresses the formation and prevention of unproductive triangles in the workplace. This chapter examines the roles of villain, victim, and rescuer in detail.

Villain Role

In your work life, you will sometimes have a negative impact on other people, either intentionally or unwittingly, through your words or actions, or by something that you fail to do. When you do not take responsibility for your negative impact, you assume the role of villain.

If you adopt the villain role in any difficult conversation, it is not likely to be successful. Villains do not work to find win/win solutions; they just want to win.

There are many behaviors which could be perceived by others as harmful or hurtful and lead to a negative impact on them. Examples include

- Shaming, blaming, or judging the behavior of others
- Making demeaning comments
- Correcting someone in front of others
- Belittling or dismissing the ideas of others
- Directing sarcasm at others
- Discriminating against or harassing others
- Yelling at others
- Withholding information
- Not consulting others on matters that concern them
- Taking sides
- Third-partying
- Gossiping about colleagues
- Being dishonest or betraying someone's trust
- Not keeping your commitments
- Giving double messages
- Attempting to control people or situations
- Rolling the eyes or using other negative body language
- Violating confidentiality
- Failing to take needed action
- Not being supportive

- Treading on relationships to accomplish tasks
- Engaging in "gotchas" or other sideways behavior
- Playing people against each other
- Manipulating others
- Leaving your work for others to do
- Comparing people
- Being competitive
- Appeasing the bad behavior of others
- Needing to win at any cost
- Trying to look good at others' expense
- Not incorporating feedback about your impact
- Not letting people know where they stand with you
- Being rigid
- Acting on unchecked assumptions
- Dodging responsibility for your mistakes
- Withdrawing to avoid conflict
- Needing to be right
- Making arbitrary decisions
- Requiring constant attention and validation
- Failing to acknowledge the contributions of others

Sometimes you can see that what you have said or done has caused a problem. At other times, you won't know unless the other person tells you. It is possible to be perceived as a villain by others and not ever know it.

When you have engaged in behavior that has been hurtful to other people, they may want to initiate a difficult conversation with you. In that case, you will be best served by being open and respectful and by taking responsibility for your impact.

If you recognize that you have done something that has offended a colleague, do not wait to be confronted. Go to the person and set it right. Even when you have made a large mistake, assuming responsibility for your impact is very disarming.

The worst things you can do are to be defensive, blame it on the other person, or deny the impact that you have had. All of these behaviors are inflammatory and will make the situation much worse. Simple errors can turn into big problems if they are not handled in a responsive, caring way.

How is it that you can have a negative impact when your intentions are good? It is necessary, but not sufficient, to have good intentions. When you act on your intentions, you need to keep paying attention to see what your actual impact has been. Sometimes you cannot discern this information without asking for feedback from the other person. You are responsible for both your intentions and your impact.

If you are given feedback that you have had a hurtful impact on someone and your response is merely that you did not intend for any harm to occur, the other person will feel dismissed and will probably be even angrier with you. To set things right with the other person, you must take responsibility for your impact and, if necessary, take corrective action.

Two of the major blocks to receiving and utilizing feedback about your impact are lack of self-esteem and pride. If you have a sense of insufficiency, it is difficult to imagine that your behavior could have a substantial influence on anyone, one way or the other. If this is true, you probably also have trouble believing that you could have much of a positive impact. You can build your capacity to receive feedback by building your sense of sufficiency.

If pride is the problem, the need to look good, be right, or feel superior will keep you from learning from your mistakes. You won't let yourself believe that you are wrong or have made a mistake. Your ego will get in the way of your taking an honest look at yourself. Letting go of pride entails learning to be compassionate with yourself and empathic with others. It means giving up perfectionism and welcoming mutuality in relationships.

Each of us has the power to be self-responsible and to communicate directly when problems arise. When we misuse that capacity and do not have difficult conversations when they are necessary, we are more likely to slide into behavior that will have a negative impact on someone else. It may seem easier to be snide, to attack, or to dodge the issue, but the results of these behaviors lead to prolonged conflict and dissatisfaction. They also make you the villain.

We all have the experience of having our words and actions misinterpreted; however, if you find that others consistently misperceive you, you would be wise to check for any blind spots you may have about your own impact. The more you are able to become conscious of your own behavior and your effect on others, the more successful you will be in your workplace interactions.

How to Stay Out of the Villain Role

The most effective way to avoid the villain role is to assume complete responsibility for your intentions toward others, your words and actions, and your impact on others. Welcome feedback and correct course when necessary. Thank those people who are willing to give you input about your negative impact. Create the change you want in your work environment by being self-responsible.

Attend to both task and relationship so that you don't create vacuums of information. Let people know where they stand with you so that they don't have to guess. Left to their own devices, they will probably make negative assumptions about your view of them.

When you find yourself in the villain role despite your best efforts, have a difficult conversation with the person who feels wronged. Apologize and make amends when necessary. Do your best to avoid repeating the behavior that caused the difficulty. We all make mistakes; it's how we handle them that shows others our true character.

> Gretchen was a middle school principal. She prided herself on making thorough decisions after considering every option. Her staff appreciated her steadiness and knew that they could count on her to do what she promised.
>
> Simon, the choir teacher, came to Gretchen with a complaint: "Gretchen, you are consistently taking so long to

approve my purchase orders that I don't have adequate time to prepare once the sheet music arrives. I would appreciate it if you could speed up the process."

Gretchen felt defensive, so she bought herself some time by saying, "Simon, I'll give this some thought and get back to you by the end of the week."

As soon as Simon left, Gretchen phoned a friend who was a principal in another district and said, "Janet, will you help me with a problem I'm having with a teacher?"

Janet agreed and Gretchen repeated her conversation with the choir teacher and asked, "What do you think?"

Janet responded, "I think Simon was very direct and respectful in the way he made his request. I wish all my teachers would do that. Does his complaint ring any bells with you? Has anyone else griped about the speed of your decision making?"

After some thought, Gretchen replied, "I think you may be on to something. Some of the art teachers have teased me about being the tortoise and not the hare. I just thought it was a joke, but now I'm thinking that they were making the same complaint in a much more indirect way. I also know that other teachers keep bugging me until I make decisions on their requests."

"So," said Janet, "putting it all together, what do you think? Is your style of stewardship having an impact on some of your teachers that you don't intend?"

"I think that might be the case," replied Gretchen.

"Do you think you need to do anything about it?" asked Janet.

"Yes," said Gretchen, "I want to make work as easy as possible for the teachers. So when they request supplies, I will ask them to give me a deadline for taking action so that I'll know when I'm creating a problem for them."

The next day, Gretchen had a brief conversation with Simon. She said, "Simon, thank you for being so direct and clear with me. I recognize that I'm making your work more stressful than it needs to be by taking such a long time to process your purchase orders, and I apologize for that. It was certainly not my intention. I am going to ask you and the rest of the staff to tell me when your orders need to be submitted so that I don't cause you difficulty in receiving the supplies you need in a timely manner. I've also expedited the orders that you have already submitted to me. Let me know how it goes, so I will know that the problem is solved."

Where we are the most gifted, we are also sometimes the most challenged. Gretchen had a talent for thoroughness, which served her well in most aspects of her job as principal. Gretchen had been unaware that her attention to detail was also causing a problem for teachers when she took too long in processing their requests for materials.

Gretchen was wise enough to ask for help when she felt reactive to Simon's complaint. Janet's questions helped Gretchen to realize that this complaint was not limited to Simon; he was simply the clearest and most direct with his concerns. Janet gently assisted Gretchen in seeing her impact and taking responsibility for changing it by asking clarifying questions, rather than giving advice.

In seeking out Janet's input, Gretchen did not form an unproductive triangle between Simon, Janet, and herself. Gretchen did not use the conversation with Janet as a way to dump on Simon or try to get Janet to take her side in a conflict with Simon. Gretchen merely asked Janet to help her see the situation clearly so that Gretchen could learn about herself and take appropriate action.

Gretchen did not need to have a lengthy difficult conversation with Simon. She only needed to apologize and let him know that she would take action to make her behavior match her intention of giving supportive assistance to her teachers. If she sticks to her new resolve, she will create a greater level of trust in her building. The teachers will see that they can count on her to be accountable for her actions. This role modeling will inspire teachers to do the same.

Gretchen avoided becoming a villain by taking action when she saw that her cautious behavior was having an impact that she did not intend. If she had not taken corrective action, her staff might have eventually come to see her as a villain as they continued to be inconvenienced. If Gretchen had fallen into the villain role, she might have arrogantly dismissed Simon's feedback, become angry with him, or even tried to blame him for the problem.

At the most extreme, villain behavior may result from a lack of empathy for others or from a fundamental desire to wield power over others for its own sake. Without empathy, it is difficult or impossible to understand the impact of one's behavior on others, so course correction may not be feasible. Those few people who live their lives to exercise their personal power at the expense of others are highly destructive in the workplace and are usually unwilling or unable to change their behavior.

Victim Role

The victim role does not have much to do with how you are treated by others. Rather, it is a disavowing of your personal efficacy in favor of unproductive behavior. If you believe that you cannot get what you need and want by communicating in a direct manner, you are likely to try to influence others in a less straightforward manner. This is a victim position.

The only reason that you cannot have the impact that you want by being plainspoken is if you are unable or unwilling to communicate your desires directly to others. You can develop your ability to be candid by learning the skills of successful difficult conversations. Your willingness to use these abilities is purely a matter of choice. If you opt for the victim role instead, you will be unreliable in difficult conversations and in your workplace relationships. Your colleagues will not be able to count on you to say what is on your mind.

The victim role can be expressed in many ways. The four that we discuss here are passivity and appeasement, personalization, strategizing, and playing the martyr.

Passivity and Appeasement

Passivity, the path of least resistance, is the opposite of proactivity. Rather than being an actor on your own behalf, you wait to be acted upon by others. You merely go with the flow, waiting for others to make important decisions that affect you.

The problem with passivity is that it puts you at the mercy of other people. When you don't like the options they select for you, you just smile and nod and act as if you are in agreement. Meanwhile, inside, you seethe and believe that someone else has done something unfair to you.

In reality, you have put yourself in this position by not participating. It's not fair to let others take the risks of decision making and then blame them when you don't like the choices they have made.

Built into passivity is the expectation that if others care about you, they should know what you want without your having to ask for it. In other words, you want people to read your mind. This expectation is not only unrealistic, but also puts others in the position of acting disrespectfully if they comply.

Trying to read someone else's mind is never appropriate. The correct response when you do not know what is going on with someone is to ask. If people frequently have to ask you what you want and need, you are not taking enough responsibility for initiating difficult conversations. Putting people in the position of having to fetch you is a form of victim behavior.

Appeasement, a variation of passivity, is the act of keeping the peace at any price. Avoiding conflict becomes more important than anything else. Even if you are being grossly mistreated, you find a way to deny what is happening to you. Left unchecked, the bad behavior of others is more likely to continue or escalate than to stop.

If you persist in this victim role of appeaser, you will begin to normalize the abnormal, and you will develop a high tolerance for deviance. You will tolerate behavior that you shouldn't. Rather than avoiding conflict, you will be absorbing it.

When you engage in the victim roles of passivity and appeasement, your underlying anger usually leads you to express your feelings aggressively. You find ways to get even with decision makers, possibly in ways that they cannot identify as coming from you. This behavior is dishonest and destructive— to you, to the other person, and to your work environment.

Walter, a high school principal, had to make a difficult decision in hiring a new assistant principal. Norma, a dean in Walter's building, had applied for the position, but he chose an outside candidate for the position instead.

Walter had decided against Norma because she had evidenced an unwillingness to engage in conflict when it was necessary. He had expressed this concern to Norma in the past, and she had not taken him up on his offer to help her find a way to gain the skills that she needed to be able to have difficult conversations.

After she was denied the promotion, Walter noticed that Norma's behavior toward him became icy. She did not smile, speak, or acknowledge his presence in any way as they passed in the halls.

When Norma's behavior had not warmed after a couple of weeks, Walter pulled her aside and said, "I'm concerned about the distance that seems to be developing between us. What's going on?"

Norma shrugged and said, "Nothing."

Walter replied, "Norma, you're not speaking to me. That isn't 'nothing.'"

She maintained, "I've just been preoccupied. Don't take it personally."

Walter responded, "I'm not taking it personally. I just want to be sure that you and I preserve our good working relationship. I value you as an important member of our team. I wonder how you're feeling about not getting the assistant principal's job."

"Oh, I'm fine with it," Norma said with a forced smile, "Really."

"Well, let me know if you want to talk."

Norma never took Walter up on his offer. She remained distant and within a few months had accepted a position in another school.

Norma was unwilling to risk telling Walter how she felt about being passed over for promotion. Even when Walter reassured Norma and invited her to talk with him, she maintained her passive victim role. Meanwhile, she was getting even with him by ignoring him. Norma's behavior reinforced Walter's opinion that he had made the right decision in choosing another candidate. He correctly believed that the ability to engage in difficult conversations and to manage conflict were essential skills for administrators.

Personalization

Personalization is an act of viewing the words and actions of others through the distorted lens of your own insufficiency. This interpretation leads you to believe that others hold the same low opinion of yourself as you do. You scrutinize other people's behavior for signs that they don't like or respect you and then blame them for the way you feel about yourself. The proof of your unworthiness, which you attribute to others, is actually based on your own unchecked assumptions. Your poor opinion of yourself is reinforced, and you become even more suspicious of others. The more you personalize, the worse it gets. It's a vicious, self-perpetuating circle.

Personalizing the behavior of others is a sophisticated way of feeling sorry for yourself and righteous at the same time. It can easily lead to self-generated despair and depression.

The truth is that most people are so busy living their own lives that they don't have the time or energy to focus on you. It is not fair or respectful to blame others for your estimation of yourself. Scrutiny of others and acting on unchecked assumptions lead to conflict.

You would be better served by putting the same energy that you use in trying to figure out what others think of you into building your sense of sufficiency and into enhancing your capacity for self-evaluation. Then, when you are concerned about the meaning of another person's behavior toward you, ask that person for the information you are missing.

Gary, an experienced first grade teacher, transferred within his district. His new principal was Tim; Gary picked Tim's building because he was reported to be an innovative leader.

Midway through the year, Gary began to feel concerned. Tim had not observed his class and had hardly seemed to notice that Gary was in the building. Gary had expected that Tim would seek him out and use his expertise. Gary began to wonder if Tim was displeased with him or if he wished he hadn't transferred.

When Gary realized he was getting in a funk about Tim, he knew it was time for a difficult conversation. Gary approached Tim one morning before school and said, "Tim, you and I haven't had much contact since I've been here. I've started to wonder if it's because you're not satisfied with what I'm doing. Before I get too carried away with that, I thought I'd better ask you directly."

With a look of surprise, Tim replied, "Why, no, Gary, quite the opposite, in fact. I'm really glad you're here. I've heard nothing but good things about your work, both in your former building and here. What would make you would think otherwise?"

Gary said, "Well, you haven't visited my class or asked me to do anything, so I just started to wonder."

"I've been trying to give you an opportunity to settle in here," replied Tim. "I have no qualms about what you are doing in your classroom. I know that changing buildings can be a bit disorienting, and I didn't want you to feel any unnecessary pressure from me. I must have overdone it."

"Let's do two things. I'd like to spend some time in your classroom next week. Then let's sit down together, and we can discuss how best to use your talents fully."

"Thanks! That sounds great," said Gary.

"I appreciate your asking me so directly for the information you needed," said Tim as he walked away.

Gary caught himself falling into the victim role of personalizing. Instead of pursuing his speculation about the meaning of Tim's behavior, he built up his courage and went directly to Tim for information.

Tim clarified his intentions and took responsibility for the impact of his behavior on Gary by scheduling a classroom observation and a one-to-one meeting with Gary. Tim also reinforced

Gary on the initiation of a difficult conversation by thanking him for coming to him directly. Gary took action that took him out of the victim role. Tim, in turn, refrained from moving into the villain role in response to Gary.

Strategizing

Strategizing is manipulating to get your way, rather than making a straightforward request for what you want and need. It is a victim position of mistrust in yourself and others.

Third-partying is one form of strategizing. Instead of going directly to a person with whom you have a problem, you tell someone else about your grievance. The object is to gain sympathy and agreement with your point of view. When you third-party, you are not seeking coaching as Gretchen did with Janet; you are gossiping and undermining the person with whom you are displeased.

An even more extreme form of strategizing is working behind the scenes to build an army of support for yourself and your opinions. Unbeknownst to the person of concern, you are third-partying with numerous people to convince them to take your side.

Not only does strategizing lack integrity, it is ineffective. You create unproductive triangles by third-partying and generate resentment in the other person when your machinations come to light. Strategizing destroys trust in the workplace and creates an unstable platform for conflict resolution.

> Daryl, the assistant superintendent for curriculum and instruction, introduced an initiative to change the way math would be taught. Daryl strongly favored a concept-driven math curriculum that would develop "number sense" so that students would learn reasoning and problem-solving skills. Daryl believed that many students could not effectively learn math with the traditional way of teaching. He toured the elementary buildings in the district, describing the math curriculum changes he wanted to propose, so that teachers and principals could have their input before he went to the school board.

Sonia, a second grade teacher, was very upset by Daryl's proposal. She favored retaining the traditional, skills-oriented way of teaching math, based on the teaching of calculations and rote memorization. Sonia thought of Daryl's proposals as "fuzzy math" and felt sure that she could not teach math that way.

Instead of voicing her concerns to Daryl, Sonia began making phone calls. She contacted her friends in several elementary schools and came up with a plan to derail Daryl's efforts to change the math curriculum. Each of the teachers in Sonia's war party was to call parents with whom they had strong working relationships and convince them to take action against Daryl's plan.

In the teachers' calls to parents, they presented only their own, traditionalist side of the math argument and tried to paint Daryl as out of touch with the classroom and children. Some of the parents who were contacted became irate and went together to the school board meeting where Daryl was to present his plan.

Daryl was completely unprepared for the protest posters and angry looks from parents that he encountered when he entered the boardroom. Although he knew that a few teachers were opposed to changing the math curriculum, he did not know that others were harboring strong feelings about his proposal without telling him. He had no idea how the parents had become involved.

After Daryl had made his presentation, several of the parents lowered their signs. At the end of the meeting they approached Daryl and apologized, saying, "We didn't really understand what this was all about. Now that we have heard what you have to say, we think maybe your ideas about math are the way to go."

"I'm happy to hear that," said Daryl. "And I'm really confused. How did you all come to be here with such strong opinions about what you thought I was going to say?"

"We're here because our children's teachers asked us to come and stop you," replied one father, and the other parents nodded. Gradually, Daryl pieced together the whole story and realized that Sonia and her co-conspirators had set him up. Daryl was very angry. He knew that he was going to have to have a series of difficult conversations. He was going to have to struggle to maintain his working relationships with the teachers who had rallied the parents against his proposal.

Daryl respectfully invited teachers to give him feedback about his proposals for change to the elementary math curriculum. Sonia and the other teachers who agreed with her did not return the respect. Rather than being direct with Daryl and engaging in public, professional discourse with him, they chose to work behind the scenes to undermine him.

It was inappropriate for the teachers to ask parents to speak for them. Every teacher who enlisted a parent to defeat Daryl formed an unproductive triangle with the teacher as victim, Daryl as the villain, and the parent as the rescuer. Teachers have great influence with parents and should not use their power in this destructive way. Not only did the teachers set Daryl up; they also set the parents up.

The teachers were perfectly capable of speaking for themselves. It was cowardly to hide behind the parents. In trying to avoid a direct clash with Daryl, they created a much larger conflict, involving parents and the school board.

Playing the Martyr

Playing the martyr is overfunctioning with an unspoken expectation of some sort of repayment. The overfunctioning might include taking on tasks you don't really want to do or accepting more than your share of the workload. It also might consist of giving gifts or doing special favors for others.

The recipients of this largesse are unaware that you are banking credits that you hope to redeem at a time of your choosing. Their payment for your overfunctioning might be accepting you or caring about you. It might also be a favor that you demand in return as your rightful due. The problem is that the other person has had no opportunity to agree or disagree. You have silently and unilaterally created a situation where the other person owes you something.

When you are playing the martyr role, you may look as if you are acting out of generosity, but that is not the case. True generosity has no expectation of repayment. This is also not the kind of martyrdom that comes from sacrificing for your dearly held beliefs or the good of others. Quite the contrary: playing the martyr is a covert act of manipulation and arrogance.

Playing the martyr creates a transactional relationship with the other person. Instead of trusting others to treat you well, you expect a trade of favors, and you keep score to make sure you get equal payment. Successful working relationships are not transactional. Instead, they rely on the good will of colleagues and on trust that everyone will receive their fair due. Trust is destroyed when relationships become transactional.

Sometimes it is easy to tell when someone is being a martyr. She may sigh heavily or whine as she agrees to do something that she really doesn't want to do. This is a rather obvious bid for sympathy and attention. At other times, you may not know that someone who appears generous is actually keeping score and waiting to collect on the debt. At first, you may like it that the other person is working so hard and making life easier and more pleasant for you. You may not be so happy when you learn that she is demanding compensation in return.

> Judith was part of a team of six high school counselors. She always volunteered to supervise the testing programs for students and spent many Saturdays administering the ACTs, SATs, or other tests. Judith received no extra pay for this duty, and her colleagues were grateful that they did not have to give up their own weekends.

> Judith also looked for opportunities to bring treats for her fellow counselors. She sometimes surprised them with lattes or homemade baked goods. When she saw a book that she thought one of her coworkers would enjoy, she bought it and left it on the person's desk with a special card.

> While the other counselors sometimes felt a little uneasy about Judith's apparent generosity, they never said anything. Mostly, they liked all of the things that she did for them.

Without telling anyone, Judith began writing a book about counseling special needs students. After she had completed a few chapters, she asked all of her colleagues if they would read what she had written and give her feedback. They readily agreed.

Judith handed out copies of her chapters and set a time for them to get together with her to talk about her book. The appointed day turned out to be a snow day, so the meeting did not take place. Without particularly thinking about it, everyone assumed that Judith would reschedule the meeting.

After a couple of weeks, the other counselors began to realize that Judith was not speaking to any of them, and there had been no lattes, special treats, or gifts. At their departmental staff meeting, they asked Judith what was bothering her.

Judith exploded, "You know very well what is bothering me. I have gone the extra mile for every one of you. I have proctored tests when I wanted to be home just like you. I have tried to be so thoughtful. I pick out special gifts for each one of you. I bring you treats. And I have never asked you for one thing until now. I was stuck in writing my book, and I asked for your help. You agreed to give me feedback, and I haven't heard from any of you. This is the one thing I've wanted from you in return for all that I've done, and you have completely let me down. I feel utterly betrayed."

After a stunned silence, one of the other counselors replied, "I'm surprised that you feel that way, Judith. I was just waiting for you to reschedule the meeting with us. I also didn't realize that you were feeling stuck in your writing. You didn't tell us that."

Another counselor chimed in, saying, "I'm uncomfortable that you seem to think that I owe you something for the things that you have done for me. If I had known that I was piling up IOUs with you, I'm not so sure I would have accepted the treats or let you handle all the testing. If I'm going to owe somebody something, I want to agree to it, not have it forced on me."

A third colleague confessed, "I think my part in this mis-understanding was not telling you that I was uncomfortable with how much you were doing for me. To be honest, I liked the treats so much that I didn't speak up out of self-interest."

A fourth counselor gently added, "I agreed to read your book and give you my feedback because I like you and respect your work, not because I thought I owed you something."

Judith said very firmly, "I do not wish to discuss this further. I do not want your help with my book, and I will never ask you for anything again."

The fifth colleague interjected, "I hope you rethink this Judith. I am still willing to help you. At the same time, I request that you stop giving me things that have strings attached."

Through gritted teeth, Judith replied, "Oh, you don't have to worry about that." Then she stalked out of the room, leaving her colleagues wide-eyed and speechless.

In one conversation, Judith managed to change her closest colleague's view of her. She revealed that she was keeping score while doing what appeared to be good deeds so that she could demand repayment. She expected the others to know what she wanted and was owed, without asking them clearly and directly for it. When they did not read her mind and comply, she exploded.

Judith's five colleagues gave her some important feedback. They objected to being beholden to Judith at her say so and asked her to stop that behavior. They admitted to having played a part in the transaction by allowing Judith to overfunction and repeatedly gift them. They let her know that their willingness to help her with her book was openhearted and not a *quid pro quo* for anything that she had given them. They invited her to re-think her position, giving her a graceful way to save face.

Unfortunately, Judith was so caught in the pattern of playing the martyr that she could not or would not drop the role. If Judith is to repair the damage that she has done with her team, she must recognize how manipulative her behavior has been, apologize to the team for her impact on them, and stop playing the martyr with them. Only then will trust be fully restored on the team.

If Judith chooses to stay angry or to act as if nothing has happened, it will be difficult for the other counselors to fully trust her in the future. They will rightly wonder what else about their interactions with Judith might be hidden from their view. This will probably cause them to cut a careful path around her. Then she will feel even more isolated and will incorrectly perceive that her colleagues are to blame. In so doing, she will complete the vicious circle of the victim role.

How to Stay Out of the Victim Role

The best way to keep from moving into the victim role is to be proactive. Assume the personal responsibility of speaking up when you don't like something. Talk directly to the person with whom you are unhappy, rather than going to a third party. This is an act of respect, to the other person and to yourself. If you believe that you are being mistreated and do not act on your own behalf, you give the person whom you view as the villain the misleading impression that his behavior is all right with you.

Own your own part of the difficulty, rather than blaming it all on the other person. Difficult interpersonal dynamics are co-created. This is actually good news, because it means that you hold half the solution to the problem. Be more committed to resolving the situation and preserving your working relationship with the other person than you are to being right and maintaining your position as a victim.

Shedding the victim role requires that you trust yourself. First, you need to learn to form your own realistic opinions of your work and your impact so that you will not be constantly at the mercy of what other people think of you. In this way, you can incorporate feedback from others, but not be ruled by it. The greater your sense of sufficiency, the more you will be able to trust yourself.

If you do not currently have good self-esteem, it is your responsibility to work to develop it. Every time you speak up for yourself, you will build your sense of sufficiency. When you remain silent or only talk to a third party, you will lower your self-esteem.

Avoiding the victim role also requires trusting others. Break the habit of making assumptions about other people's motivations and intentions. Do not act on unchecked assumptions as if they were facts. Ask for information when you can't tell what's happening. Do not assume that other people's unproductive behavior is about you—it is actually about them.

You are responsible for your own happiness in life. You are at risk if you depend on others or on circumstances to bring you joy. Looking outside of yourself for fulfillment is a victim stance.

Direct more of your attention to what is working rather than dwelling on the negative. There is almost always more that is working than is going wrong. When you see a problem, raise it and offer at least three possible solutions, rather than waiting for someone else to fix the situation for you.

Assume responsibility for managing your feelings, rather than letting them run you. If you are angry, channel your emotion responsibly into direct communication and problem solving. Don't indulge in being reactive. Allow your emotional wounds to heal, rather than continually reopening them. This will prevent you from holding resentments that pollute your interior life.

Do not volunteer for activities in which you actually do not want to participate. Keep transactions out of your relationships. Act from an open heart, rather than as part of an unspoken deal to get what you want. Assume that you can get what you need and want from others by asking in a straightforward manner. Do not expect others to read your mind. Give them the information that they need.

Embrace adversity—it can be your greatest teacher if you allow yourself to learn from it. There are many times in your life when you won't like the situation in which you find yourself. It is how you respond in these times that will determine whether or not you adopt the victim role. Learn the lessons from your difficult experiences, so you won't have to keep repeating them.

Look for role models of people who refused to be victims, even when they were faced with great adversity. It is inspiring to learn about ordinary people who rose to greatness through such courage. Some of them are famous, and others are working right alongside of you. Learn about their lives, and find out how they stay out of the victim role. Here are four such people:

- *Desmond Tutu* quit his job as a teacher in protest when the repressive government of South Africa ordained a deliberately inferior system of education for black students. He went on to become an Anglican priest and Bishop of Johannesburg and win the Nobel Peace Prize. During the dark days of apartheid, Bishop Tutu never lost his joy—he kept singing and dancing throughout and helped others to maintain their hope. Never adopting the victim role allowed him to play a healing part in the Truth and Reconciliation Commission in post-apartheid South Africa.

- *Rosa Parks* attended the Alabama State Teachers' College, but was working as a seamstress in racially segregated Montgomery, Alabama, in 1955. At the end of a tiring workday, she calmly declined to give up her seat on a public bus to a white passenger and was arrested for violating a city ordinance. Rosa Parks' refusal to be a victim launched the civil rights movement in the United States. Today, through the Rosa and Raymond Parks Institute for Self Development, she passes on her tradition of courage, dignity, and commitment to young people.

- *Jaime Escalante* was a high school teacher in La Paz, Bolivia, when he immigrated to California at the age of 33. He could speak no English and discovered that he would have to begin all over again and get another college degree in order to qualify to teach in the United States. Instead of feeling sorry for himself, he took a job as a janitor in a restaurant and began the long journey to becoming certified as a teacher. At age 43, he began teaching math to Latino students in a failing high school in East Los Angeles. Soon, he inspired those young people to shed their own victim attitudes and succeed in advanced placement courses. He has been recognized in many ways as an outstanding teacher, including being the recipient of a United States Presidential Medal.

♦ *Ann Bancroft* never let her severe dyslexia keep her from her dreams. First she earned a college degree and became a teacher and coach. Then she shattered the notion that women were too weak to be polar explorers by becoming the first woman to cross both the north and south poles. Ann Bancroft was named one of the Remarkable Women of the Twentieth Century. She helps other women and girls to fulfill their courageous dreams through the Ann Bancroft Foundation. Ann Bancroft never had time to be a victim.

Each of these four people did not make just one decision to avoid the victim role. Every day they had to decide to not give in to passivity, appeasement, personalizing, strategizing, and martyrdom. They did not collapse under the weight of discrimination, racism, poverty, starting over, or learning disabilities.

On the contrary, they maintained their dignity and integrity. They were consistently proactive rather than reactive. They did not allow themselves to be limited by circumstances or the behavior of others. All four of them looked for ways to help others to transcend their circumstances and accomplish their dreams. With an attitude of abundance, they believed that there was enough for everyone.

Most of us lapse into the victim role occasionally. For others, the victim stance becomes a way of life. Perpetual victims are constantly scanning for ways that others are victimizing them. They never let old resentments die and keep reopening emotional wounds. They feel the power in being a victim and control others through helplessness and blame. They ask for help, but really only want attention. You can spin in circles trying to come to their aid, but nothing will ever be enough for them. Underneath it all, they do not want to take responsibility for their own actions and impact—they want to blame everything on someone else. This is very toxic behavior in the workplace.

Rescuer Role

In the rescuer role, you compound the problem between the victim and the villain by making it easier for the victim to avoid dealing with the villain. The only way a conflict can be resolved is for the person who is dissatisfied to talk directly to the colleague in question. If the injured party is talking to you instead, you are in the way of a resolution. You may become the rescuer by listening to repeated complaints about the villain, taking sides with the victim, or attempting to act for the victim.

If someone approaches you in the victim role, you may be tempted to simply lend a sympathetic ear and listen to complaints about the villain. This misplaced helpfulness may seem harmless, but it is not. It is very possible that the victim will blow off enough steam in venting to you that he will no longer feel compelled to take action with the perceived villain. With the edge taken off of his anger, the victim will temporarily feel better and experience the illusion that the problem is solved.

If you rescue by listening repeatedly to a victim's complaints, you become a garbage can for his junk. This enables the victim to avoid assuming personal responsibility for solving his own problems. It also sours your view of your workplace with issues that may not even concern you. Being a repository for others' negative feelings elevates your stress level artificially.

When you enter the rescuer role by taking sides with the victim, you are on very dangerous ground. Usually, you have heard only one side of the story and have made negative assumptions about the villain based on the hearsay of the victim. You don't even know if there has been a simple misunderstanding or if there is a real problem. When you take sides in a conflict, you make it more difficult for anyone to find a resolution, and you become a part of the problem.

When a victim refuses to approach the perceived villain directly, it may be tempting to try to talk to the villain for the victim. This form of rescuing is bound to put the villain on the defensive. It is immediately apparent that you and the victim have been third-partying, which is enough to make anyone feel angry and suspicious. In order to resolve the issue, the villain and victim will need to have an exchange of perspectives. They can only do that directly—not with you in the way.

Rescuer behaviors are disrespectful to both the victim and the villain. The unspoken message you give to the victim is that you believe the victim is unable to handle him- or herself in difficult situations and is incapable of having a successful difficult conversation. The implied negative assumption about the villain is that you believe the villain is so untrustworthy that it would be pointless to have a difficult conversation with him or her.

Underneath the rescuer role is an arrogant attitude that you are superior to both of the other parties. You can handle difficulty and they can't. As a rescuer, you undermine both the villain and the victim. This may not be your conscious intention, but it is your impact.

The rescuer is a role that does not require vulnerability—you get to look good without risking anything. Juxtaposed against the villain role, you look like the hero. Playing rescuer requires a villain.

Assuming the role of the white knight can be very seductive. It may give you a false feeling of self-worth to ride in and save the day. The problem is that you are doing it at the expense of the other two people.

> Samantha and Julian were speech pathologists serving several schools within a district. Samantha came to Julian to complain about their supervisor. "I'm so frustrated with Harry. He keeps scheduling my school visits too close together. I can't get from one school to another on time."
>
> Julian asked, "What does Harry say about it?"
>
> "Oh, I can't talk to Harry. He's so gruff. I feel intimidated by him," said Samantha.

"I know what you mean. I used to feel that way about him, too. He's hard to handle," replied Julian.

"Would you talk to him for me, Julian?" requested Samantha. "I think he might listen to you."

Julian beamed and stood up taller: "Sure, Samantha, I'll talk to him for you."

Julian approached Harry the next morning, saying, "Samantha is having trouble getting from one student appointment to another. Apparently, you're scheduling her visits too close together. Can you give her a break and space them out a little more?"

Harry scowled, "If Samantha is having a problem, why are you talking to me? Where is she? The two of you must have been talking about me. What did you tell her about me—that I'm such an ogre she can't talk to me herself?"

"I can easily fix the scheduling snafu, but now we have a bigger problem. Samantha must be able to talk to me directly, and I want you to stay out of problems that don't concern you. Right now I don't feel very good about either one of you. I want both of you in my office after school."

Julian succumbed to rescuing Samantha from Harry, thus entering the role of rescuer. Julian listened to Samantha's complaints about Harry, sided with her negative view of Harry, and agreed to act for her. He held an inflated view of himself as he went to confront Harry. Essentially, Julian was using both Samantha and Harry to feel good about himself.

Julian's high was short-lived because Harry was justifiably angry with both Julian and Samantha. Julian's actions turned a simple situation into a much more complex problem. Samantha set Julian up by requesting that he play an inappropriate role, but Julian bears the responsibility for complying. Julian could have played a constructive role and avoided becoming a rescuer by coaching Samantha to have her own difficult conversation with Harry. Unfortunately, that is not the option he chose.

How to Stay Out of the Rescuer Role

When a victim approaches you to talk about a villain, you have a choice about whether to enter the rescuer role or not. You can show empathy and caring for the person who approaches you in the victim role without trying to come to the rescue.

Here are the types of responses that will keep you out of the rescuer role while preserving your relationship with the person who has assumed the victim role. The situation is this: *Jo is angry because of a decision your mutual principal, Shelly, made and comes to you to grumble about Shelly. You might reply:*

- *What did Shelly say when you told her what you thought?*
- *I'm sorry you had a bad experience, and I don't want to get in the middle between you and Shelly.*
- *I have faith in your ability to go and have a difficult conversation about this with Shelly.*
- *I've had to say some difficult things to Shelly in the past, and I have found her to be receptive to my feedback.*
- *Shelly's not here, and it seems as if we're gossiping about her. I wouldn't like it if someone talked about me behind my back.*
- *Jo, you're talking to the wrong person. I can't solve this problem with you. You need to talk to Shelly.*
- *I'm not sure what your intention is in telling me about this. Do you want me to take sides with you against Shelly?*
- *You seem to be taking this very personally. What buttons has this situation with Shelly pushed for you?*
- *I'll be happy to do a role-play with you so that you can get ready to talk to Shelly about your concerns.*
- *Jo, you're sounding like a victim. That's not how I see you. I know that you are capable of standing up for yourself.*
- *Maybe your mentor could coach you about how to approach Shelly about this.*
- *My experience is that I usually have played some part when I have a problem with someone. Do you have any*

idea how you might have contributed to this situation with Shelly? What's your part?

♦ *Jo, you've come to me several times lately complaining about Shelly. For my sake and yours, I can't listen to you complain about her anymore. I feel as if I will become a part of the problem if I continue to listen to you gripe about her. I don't want to be an enabler. Besides, it's depressing to listen to the same complaints over and over again.*

♦ *How can I support you in having a conversation with Shelly about this?*

♦ *What is it that you'd like from me about this?*

♦ *No, I won't talk to Shelly for you. I think that would be insulting to both of you.*

♦ *Yes, I might consider going with you to talk to Shelly. I would want to make it clear to both of you that I am just a neutral observer and will not be taking sides.*

♦ *Stop. As much as I care about you, I just can't listen to this.*

Any of these types of responses would keep you out of the rescuer role. They set limits while showing caring and empathy. Some of these replies ask Jo to take responsibility for herself or look at her own part in her conflict with Shelly.

Some people become addicted to the role of rescuer. They may be so busy speaking for others that you have no idea where they stand personally. They love the feeling of control they get from minimizing the villain and the victim and the high they get from being a hero. These people may even create conflict so that they can star as the knight in shining armor who comes to the rescue. They use other people to make themselves feel good.

Usually, these people do not want to give up the rescuer role and may become very vindictive if they are exposed. If that is the case, it may work to isolate them. If nobody will play the victim or the villain, they will have nowhere to go with the rescuer role.

Chapter Summary

The villain, the victim, and the rescuer always create havoc in the workplace. People acting in these roles destroy trust within the organization and make successful difficult conversations impossible. Staying out of all three roles is an act of personal responsibility and respect.

Villains cause a negative impact on others, either intentionally or unintentionally. When confronted with their impact, villains have the choice to accept personal responsibility and change their behavior, which will take them out of the villain role.

The victim gives up personal power in favor of unproductive behavior. Victims personalize the behavior of others. Instead of being proactive, victims try to get their needs met by being passive and by appeasing villainous behavior, strategizing covertly with colleagues, or playing the martyr. Giving up the victim role requires a sense of personal sufficiency and a willingness to be proactive rather than reactive.

The rescuer gets in the way of the resolution of the problem between the victim and the villain by enabling the victim in some way. The rescuer may be a sympathetic ear for the victim, may actively take sides with the victim, or may even attempt to act on behalf of the victim. The rescuer's behavior is demeaning to both the victim and the villain. The way to shed the rescuer role is to support the other two parties in dealing with each other directly.

Chapter 5

Unproductive Triangles in the Workplace

There are many successful threesomes at work in education.

- ◆ Three colleagues team-teaching fourth grade
- ◆ A high school principal working with two assistants
- ◆ A team of three social workers serving several schools
- ◆ A pool of three secretaries in a business office
- ◆ Members of a school board, administration, and the teachers' union coming together to pass a bonding referendum

These triads are productive triangles. All three of the individuals or groups in a productive triangle are self-responsible and have respect for the other members. All parties work to maintain clear communications and have difficult conversations when they are needed. Everyone works together to successfully accomplish tasks, while maintaining positive working relationships.

In contrast, in unproductive triangles in the workplace, there are breakdowns in self-responsibility, communication, and respect. Tasks are not accomplished well or may not be done at all. Relationships become tangled and problematic. Difficult conversations do not occur. The parties feel disrespected and disgruntled.

What Is an Unproductive Triangle?

An unproductive triangle is one in which all three roles of victim, villain, and rescuer are present. Either individuals or groups can play all three roles. Usually, unproductive triangles emerge when someone believes that he has been mistreated in some way and does not have a difficult conversation with the person who he believes has treated him badly. Instead, he goes to a third person and complains about how he was treated. In doing so, he has assigned himself the victim role. The person who he believes mistreated him is relegated to the villain, role and the third party is brought on board in the rescuer role.

> Jim was a first-year teacher who was excited to be part of the social studies department in a large high school. When the department chair announced in October that the social studies curriculum would be updated for the following year, Jim volunteered to be on the committee that was to make recommendations for changes in the course offerings.

> At the first meeting of the committee, Jim proposed a new class about the rights and responsibilities of voting. After the meeting, Bert, a 22-year veteran of the social studies department told Jim, "Son, you don't know squat about teaching yet. You should be quiet and pay attention, and you might learn something."

> Jim was shocked and offended, but did not reply to Bert. That night, Jim called his friend Susan, who was also in the social students department, but not on the committee. "You're not going to believe what happened to me," Jim said, and he proceeded to tell her what Bert had said to him. Susan was very sympathetic with Jim, and they dissected Bert for half an hour.

Bert was clearly out of line in pulling rank and trying to silence Jim, the newcomer. It was a misuse of Bert's years of experience, and it was disrespectful to Jim. Bert cast himself in the role of villain. Instead of responding directly to Bert, Jim put himself in the role of victim and went to a third party. This choice disempowered Jim and disrespected Bert by talking about him behind his back. Susan put herself in the rescuer role by colluding with Jim. In letting Jim work off steam about his encounter with Bert, she made it possible for him to feel as though he had resolved the problem, when, in fact, he had just taken the edge off his feelings. Jim felt better enough after talking with Susan that dealing with Bert directly did not seem so compelling.

After all of this expenditure of energy, the problem still exists between Jim and Bert. Jim doesn't even know what Bert's intention was in making his remark. The only way this situation can be resolved is for Jim to have a difficult conversation with Bert.

A person in any of the three roles in an unproductive triangle—victim, villain, or rescuer—can prevent the triangle from forming or dismantle an unproductive triangle once it is in place. There is no such thing as a one- or two-sided triangle.

Bert could have stayed out of the villain role and kept from becoming the first leg of the triangle by not talking in an arrogant, dismissive manner to Jim. He could have treated him as an adult and as part of the department.

Jim could have said, "Bert, I'm surprised by your tone. It makes me wonder if I'm coming across as a smart alec. I have a deep respect for all of the work that you and others have done in the social studies department. I know that I have a lot to learn from you. I also hope that you will be open to my ideas. I want to be an active part of this faculty." This way of dealing with Bert would have left Jim feeling empowered rather than victimized. It would have given Bert an opportunity to set the situation right and to become an ally for Jim in the department.

It takes three parties to create an unproductive triangle. Susan could have prevented the triangle from forming, even if Jim had come to her to third-party about Bert, by directing Jim back to Bert. She might have said, "Jim, I know that you're angry at Bert, and I don't blame you, but I'm not the person you need to be talking to about this. The only way you can resolve this situation is to talk with Bert directly."

Role Confusion—Who's the Victim?

Sometimes two of the three parties in an unproductive triangle both see themselves as the victims. This adds further confusion to the already complex unproductive triangle.

After a rough first year of teaching seventh grade language arts, Chad was assigned a mentor. Chad's principal, Richard, picked Bernice for the job because she was a seasoned teacher with strong skills in both the English curriculum and classroom management. Bernice spent three mornings a week working side-by-side with Chad in his classroom. Bernice gave Chad feedback on his performance and suggestions for further effectiveness.

A month into this new mentoring relationship, Chad went to Richard to complain about Bernice. "I don't like how this mentorship is going. Bernice is so critical that much of the time I don't feel like I'm doing anything right. Can't you find someone who knows how to give feedback in a more constructive way? I need to hear what I did right before I can listen to what I did wrong. I felt better about my teaching when I was struggling along on my own."

Richard responded, "Let me talk to Bernice."

Richard phoned Bernice and repeated Chad's complaint about her and asked her if she could be more positive with Chad. Bernice replied, "First, I have given Chad lots of positive feedback. I just don't do it every time I give him a suggestion about how to be more effective. When the class is beginning to get away from him, it's not feasible for me to start with a compliment.

"Second, Chad isn't improving because he can't handle anything but positive input. He seems to shrivel if there is any hint that he hasn't performed perfectly. He seems to want approval rather than actual mentoring.

"Third, at least twice a week I have asked Chad how he thought the mentoring relationship was going. He has consistently told me that he is getting a lot out of it. Now, I find out that he has taken his complaints to you instead. I feel stabbed in the back. Richard, you've got to take disciplinary action against Chad so he knows he can't get away with this kind of behavior."

Chad's need to be perfect kept him from incorporating any of the challenging feedback from Bernice. Instead, he blamed his feelings of inadequacy on Bernice. This internal dynamic anchored him into the victim role, with Bernice as the villain. Chad could have escaped the victim role by talking directly to Bernice about his feelings. Instead, Chad turned to Richard to rescue him.

There were several ways that Richard could have stayed out of the rescuer role. He could have expressed his faith in Bernice as a mentor and insisted that Chad look again at her feedback. Richard could have let Chad know that his formula for receiving feedback was unrealistic. Richard also could have asked to meet with Chad and Bernice together to work out the difficulties in their mentoring relationship. Instead, Richard chose to speak to Bernice for Chad—a classic rescuer response.

Bernice also felt as though she had been wronged by Chad talking to Richard about her rather than coming to her directly. She felt betrayed by Richard's attempt to rescue Chad. In her view of the triangle, she was the victim, and Chad was the villain. She also then asked Richard to discipline Chad, making Richard the rescuer in her version of the triangle.

There are several additional consequences from this unproductive triangle. The relationships between Chad and Bernice and between Richard and Bernice have been weakened, and it will be harder for them to trust each other in the future. It also will be more difficult to resolve the mentoring issues between Chad and Bernice so that Chad gets the help he needs. Chad will probably be less willing to listen to Bernice because Richard has taken his side, validating Chad's complaints about Bernice.

In addition, Richard, who will make the final decision about whether to retain Chad at the end of his probationary period, will have less information about Chad because he did not look closely enough at this situation. Bernice, who is from a pool of district-wide mentors, will be less likely to agree to work with Richard's teachers in the future, knowing that she cannot count on Richard to support her. A fairly simple problem has become a complicated mess.

Preventing Unproductive Triangles

Since it takes all three roles—victim, villain, and rescuer—to form an unproductive triangle, any one person can prevent its formation. From each of the three roles, a different approach is needed to stay out of the triangle.

When you believe that you have been victimized, the way to avoid participating in an unproductive triangle is to have a difficult conversation with the person whose behavior you do not like. This is the only way to stay out of the victim role and the only way to resolve the conflict. Do not go to a third party for commiseration or to build an army of support for your own position.

To avoid becoming the villain, it is essential to take responsibility for the impact of your words and actions. Conduct yourself in a manner that is respectful, clear, and direct. Be aware of your intentions toward others. Welcome difficult conversations about your impact. When you receive feedback that you have had a negative impact on someone, whether you intended it or not, own your part of the problem. If necessary, take remedial action to correct the situation. Do your best not to repeat the behavior that led to the other person feeling harmed or hurt.

You can avoid the rescuer role in a number of ways. Do not allow yourself to be on the receiving end of gossip. If someone comes to you to complain about a third party, send that person back to the source. Do not speak or act for other competent adults who believe that they have been wronged. Refuse to take sides. Instead, encourage people in conflict to have difficult conversations with each other.

Triangle Cultures

In workplaces where avoiding difficult conversations is the norm, many unproductive triangles are created. When this situation endures over a long period of time, a toxic organizational environment develops. When that happens, a triangle culture is born.

A triangle culture is created by the absence of difficult conversations and leads to a breakdown in the organization and to other predictable patterns of unproductive behavior. Here are the characteristics of a triangle culture:

◆ More time and energy are spent on negativity than on finding creative solutions.

◆ The focus is on what's not working rather than on what is working.

◆ Whining and complaining are reinforced with attention.

◆ Battle lines have been drawn, and those on opposite sides view the others as the enemy.

◆ Colleagues bond around their unproductive patterns rather than their character, strengths, and talents.

◆ The employee's lounge feels like an emotional cesspool.

◆ People do not feel valued.

◆ Someone is singled out as the scapegoat and is held responsible for what is wrong in the work environment.

◆ Gossiping and third-partying abound.

◆ Trust is nonexistent.

◆ Problems never die—ancient history feels current.

◆ Fear is cultivated, not managed.

◆ Differences are viewed with suspicion.

◆ People dread coming to work.

◆ Reactivity is acted on, not managed.

- Blaming others replaces self-responsibility.
- Illnesses and absences increase.
- Unchecked assumptions are rampant and treated as facts.
- Creativity and learning are stifled.
- Power is misused.
- Passive-aggressive behavior is tuned to a fine art.
- Tasks are not accomplished in an effective, timely manner.
- People become cynical and jaded.
- Turnover is high.
- Conflicts are not resolved.
- Leaders are not respected.

Does this sound like a place you would like to work?

Chuck, a superintendent, received a surprise visit from eight teachers from one of his elementary schools. They had come to complain about their principal, David. The teachers told Chuck that the working environment in their school had deteriorated, and they blamed David for it. They said that the faculty was divided into factions, and it was difficult to get agreement on anything. The teachers complained that David micromanaged them and did not respect them as competent professionals. They accused David of having favorites on the staff and siding with them in conflicts. In the end, the teachers asked Chuck to fire David.

Chuck listened to the delegation and then asked if they had aired their grievances with David. One of the teachers replied, "Oh, it's impossible to have a constructive conversation with David," and the others nodded.

Chuck picked up his calendar and said, "I want to bring you all back when David can be present for the discussion. Let's reconvene on Wednesday after school, and I will arrange for David to be here."

The teachers shifted in their seats, and one of them said, "We don't want David to know that we came to see you.

We're afraid that he'll retaliate. Can't you just handle this and keep our names out of it?"

"No, I won't do that. You have raised some serious concerns. In order to get to the bottom of them, we all need to be in the same room. I'll see you on Wednesday."

Chuck did not want David to be blind-sided in the meeting with the teachers. So before the Wednesday meeting, Chuck scheduled a private conversation with David and laid out the gist of the teachers' complaints and told him who would be attending the meeting.

In response, David waved his hand dismissively, "Oh, those people—the chronic malcontents. Nothing I do ever satisfies them. They're right that the atmosphere in our building isn't the greatest, but it's their doing. They are the problem, but they always want to blame it on me. Maybe we should split them up and transfer some of them to other buildings. You'll back me up in the meeting, right?"

Chuck replied, "I will always support your leadership, and I want you to be open to hearing what these teachers have to say. I am concerned that you simply want to blame them and get rid of them. That's a mirror of their attitude toward you. In my experience, when the environment in a building becomes negative, everyone bears part of the responsibility and holds part of the solution."

The group of teachers who came to complain viewed themselves as David's victims, and they wanted Chuck to rescue them. Fortunately, Chuck was thinking more complexly than that and refused to play the rescuer role. He would not let the teachers hide behind him and scheduled a meeting that would put all of the parties together in one room.

From the teachers' comments, Chuck was concerned that a triangle culture had formed in their building. When he talked privately with David, his fears were confirmed, and he could see the principal's part in the problem. David viewed himself as the victim of the dissident teachers. Chuck understood that no one could lead effectively from the victim position.

Preventing Triangle Cultures

It is possible to dismantle triangle cultures and restore workplace vibrancy; however, it is much easier to take action to keep triangles from forming. The best way to prevent triangle cultures is to establish clear agreements within the organization about how you will treat each other.

If possible, these group norms should be discussed and agreed upon by the entire work group. Then each person should be asked to uphold the code. Here is a sampling of agreements to consider including.

- When I have an issue with someone in the organization, I commit to initiating a conversation with that person within a week.

- I will speak and act with respect toward my colleagues, avoiding shaming and blaming others and myself.

- I will not gossip about colleagues or a third party when I have an issue with someone.

- I will check assumptions that I have about colleagues before acting on them.

- I will not receive gossip or participate in anyone else's attempt to third-party.

- I will be open to both positive and negative feedback.

- I will be accountable for my words and actions and will take responsibility for my impact on others.

- When I see a problem, I will bring it forward with at least three possible solutions.

- I will create value for myself in my work life.

- I will help to create a place at the table for everyone in the organization, especially those with whom I disagree.

Of all the things that you can do to create a healthy environment in your workplace, keeping the lines of communication open is the most important. Respectful difficult conversations, which are devoid of blame and judgment, are essential. Talk it out!

It is possible that some people in your workplace will not adhere to the guidelines you agree on as a group. They may continue to engage in negative behaviors and may attempt to initiate unproductive triangles. It is important to treat these individuals with respect and not to ostracize or scapegoat them, while at the same time not participating in their destructive conduct. Set clear, firm limits on their behavior and work to maintain your compassion for them.

Facilitated Difficult Conversations

When two parties cannot seem to hear or understand each other, it might be helpful to have a facilitator present. In order to be helpful, a facilitator should be neutral and must scrupulously avoid becoming a rescuer so that an unproductive triangle is not formed.

The primary role of a facilitator is to be a fair witness to a difficult conversation. A successful facilitator is fully present during the interaction and maintains compassion for both sides. This behavior helps to create a safe environment in which to resolve the conflict.

The two people in conflict should agree upon the facilitator. It is an honor to be asked to be a facilitator for a difficult conversation. It means that both parties trust you to remain neutral.

If you are asked to facilitate a difficult conversation, there are several questions you should ask yourself before agreeing to play the role. Am I truly a neutral party in this conflict? Do I have any investment in the outcome? Am I reactive to either party or to the subject matter of the discord? Will I be able to stay fully present for both people during the conversation? Can I avoid forming a triangle by staying out of the rescuer role? Do I have the time and energy to be the facilitator, and do I want to do it? If you need to say "no," it is important to do so clearly, directly, and respectfully.

If you do agree to facilitate, there are several things to avoid. It is not your role to set up the conversation between the two people. To do so would lead you into the rescuer role. They should talk to each other directly. It is also not part of your role as facilitator to attempt to solve the problem for the two parties or to fix either one of them. You will not be taking sides or declaring a winner.

As a facilitator, you role is to help look for win/win options. You will be most effective if you are rooting for a mutually satisfactory solution to the problem. Assume that both people want to work through the problem, even if the process might not be completely comfortable for them. They want to restore their working relationship or they wouldn't be there.

Before the conversation takes place, review the principles in this book. Take the time to remember what you value about each of the parties and to notice what they have in common. Think about how you can help to create a safe atmosphere for the upcoming conversation.

During the conversation, listen carefully. If you think that the two people might be saying the same thing in different words, ask them if this is the case. If necessary, make observations that using inflammatory language, shaming, blaming, or judging might be making it difficult for them to hear each other. If you think that they are not incorporating aspects of successful difficult conversations, steer them into more productive territory.

It is possible that you will not have to actively do or say anything as the facilitator. Your presence may be all that is needed. People will often take more responsibility for what they say and do if a neutral witness is present.

After you facilitate the difficult conversation, let go of any attachment to the outcome. The behavior of the two parties and the outcome are not within your control. You are only responsible for your own thoughts and behavior.

It is essential that you keep confidential everything that you witness as a facilitator. If you reveal this information to anyone else, you will have created an unproductive triangle. Anything about the conversation that is shared with others should be agreed upon by the two parties and should come from them, not you.

Chapter Summary

An unproductive triangle is one in which all three roles of victim villain, and rescuer are present. Instead of talking directly with the perceived villain, the victim turns to a third party to be rescued. In some cases, the villain may also feel like a victim, mistrusting the intentions of the person who has been operating behind his back.

Any of the three parties can prevent a triangle from forming. The victim can go directly to the person who she believes has wronged her. The villain can assume responsibility for his impact, even if he intended no harm. The potential rescuer can decline to play the role by not engaging with the victim and sending her back to the villain.

In work environments where difficult conversations are not the norm, many unproductive triangles form as people attempt to avoid conflict. In some cases, this avoidance leads to a heavy, toxic work environment—a triangle culture, which breeds negativity.

To prevent a triangle culture from forming, it is important to reach agreements about how colleagues will treat each other. Maintaining a healthy work environment takes commitment and vigilance on the part of most of the staff.

When two parties are not being successful with their difficult conversation, a facilitator might help. The role of the facilitator is to be neutral and help to find a win/win solution. If the facilitator remains a fair witness to the process, a productive triangle will be formed. On the other hand, if the facilitator falls into the trap of assuming the rescuer role, an unproductive triangle will result.

SECTION THREE

SUCCESSFUL DIFFICULT CONVERSATIONS

Chapter 6

Preparing for a Difficult Conversation

Preparing for a difficult conversation is a process of clarifying your own thoughts and feelings about a problem before you approach the other person who is involved in the situation. The clearer you are, the more likely it is that the difficult conversation will be successful.

Preparation, in this context, is different from rehearsal. Being well prepared means that you know exactly where you stand on the issues, which helps you to organize your thinking and allows you to be articulate.

Rehearsing means practicing what you are going to say, word for word. The problem with writing a script for the conversation is that the other person does not have a copy. As soon as he opens his mouth to respond, your detailed plans no longer work. Rehearsing also can make you sound canned and insincere. If you try to stick to your agenda, the other person is likely to feel that you are trying to control the conversation, which will be an accurate perception.

It is a leap of faith to trust in your own clarity. Preparing yourself for a difficult conversation allows you to be yourself, in the moment. This assists you in maintaining your curiosity and compassion for the other person, two conditions that are necessary for finding win/win solutions. This chapter takes you through a series of questions that prepares you for a difficult conversation. The examples follow one teacher through the process of preparation.

The Process of Preparation

What's Bothering You?

You usually know when something or someone is bothering you, but it's not always so easy to pinpoint exactly what the issue is. In order to have a successful difficult conversation, you need to be as specific as possible about what you see as the problem. If you only talk in generalities, the other person will not know what the problem really is and will not be able to do anything about it.

Bill, a middle school special education teacher, was chairing a committee which had the mission of improving the effectiveness of special education teachers and regular classroom teachers in working together to help students. Bill found himself increasingly annoyed during the meetings with Ann, a science teacher, but he had not stopped to think about why. He knew that other members of the committee also found her tiresome. He decided to keep track of his reactions to Ann in the next meeting so that he could figure out exactly what was bothering him.

What Bill noticed in the following meeting was that Ann talked as much as all the other committee members put together. When she had the floor, Ann made the same points repeatedly, and Bill watched the other members' eyes glaze over she talked. Bill was surprised to find that he found Ann's ideas to be creative and workable. He realized that what was annoying was the way she dominated the conversation and said the same things over and over again. Everyone on the committee, including himself, tended to ignore Ann's ideas because of her style.

If all Bill knew was that Ann annoyed him, he could not have a successful difficult conversation with Ann about her behavior in the committee meeting. Now that he knows his annoyance with Ann stems from her dominating the conversation and repeating herself, he can address the problem constructively with Ann.

When and How Did This Situation Begin?

If you can trace the history of the problem, you usually can gain valuable information that will help you to find a mutually workable solution. It's easier to make necessary changes if you know what triggered the problem in the first place.

> Bill thought back over the five meetings of the committee. He realized that the members had become more and more dismissive of Ann. They had started by fidgeting when she talked and moved to looking away when she spoke. In the last meeting there had been overt eye rolling. When she finished talking, no one responded, and the subject was changed. It was as if she had not spoken at all. Historically, the more the group ignored Ann, the more airtime she used. She kept trying harder and harder to be heard, without realizing that she was having the opposite effect of what she wanted.

By tracing the history of the problem, Bill was able to see that the group had become locked in a covert power struggle with Ann. Both sides kept doing more and more of the same behaviors and expecting different results.

What's Your Source of Information?

How do you know what you know about the problem? Is it through direct observation, by using your intuition, or is it by the report of someone else?

> Much of Bill's information about the problem came from his direct observation of Ann's behavior in committee meetings. He could see that she talked more than anyone else and repeated herself. Some of the committee members had made comments to Bill outside of the meetings

that they felt frustrated with Ann and wondered if he could manage to remove her from the committee. Bill also guessed intuitively that additional members of the committee were also annoyed about Ann because of their body language when she spoke.

Evaluating the sources of information that you have employed in thinking about the problem will help you to sort out what you actually know first hand, where you have made assumptions, and where you are simply relying on someone else's experiences and opinions. We create the biggest messes when we reach conclusions based on unchecked assumptions and third-party reports and then act on those conclusions.

What Assumptions Have You Made about the Other Person?

An assumption is a conjecture about the meaning of someone else's words, actions, and body language. Assumptions can be positive or negative. Two different people may behave in the same way toward you, but you may arrive at opposite assumptions about their actions. For example, if a friend interrupts you while you are talking, you may attribute his behavior to excitement. On the other hand, if someone you do not like interrupts, you may assume that he is being arrogant.

However an assumption is arrived at, it is just a guess. Even if you are gifted intuitively, you may still be wrong. It is disrespectful to act on assumptions about others without checking with them directly to see if your hypotheses are correct.

Bill sorted out three sets of assumptions that he had unconsciously made about the committee situation. First were his assumptions about Ann. Bill recognized that he had made negative assumptions about her: she wasn't a team player; she just wanted her way and didn't care about anyone else; she was oblivious to others' responses to her.

Second, Bill had assumed that the nonverbal cues from other committee members (fidgeting, looking away, eye rolling) meant that they all agreed with his negative assumptions about Ann. Finally, Bill also realized that he assumed that the whole committee saw him as an ineffective leader because he had not done anything about Ann's behavior.

Of the three sets of assumptions that Bill made, the most dangerous one was that he thought that the committee did not approve of his leadership. When you feel that your flaws have been publicly exposed, you are susceptible to resorting to your worst behavior in reaction.

How Do You Feel about the Other Person and the Situation?

Identifying your feelings will help you take responsibility for these emotional reactions when you have a difficult conversation. Any feeling you have, no matter how strong, is acceptable. What you do with that feeling may or may not be suitable. The stronger the feeling, the more you will have to work with yourself to act responsibly. How you act in response to your feelings is a choice. Exercising this choice is only possible if you are aware of how you are feeling.

> Bill assessed his feelings about Ann and found that he was frustrated and angry with her and that he was beginning to actively dislike her. Bill also found that he was feeling embarrassed by Ann's behavior and strongly wanted it to stop before he felt humiliated about his leadership of the committee.
>
> Bill winced when he remembered that in the last meeting of the committee he had said sarcastically to Ann, "Are you finished?" after she had spoken at length. He knew himself well enough to realize that he was on the verge of behaving even more inappropriately if he did not manage his feelings. He also knew that he needed to have a difficult conversation with Ann soon, or his feelings would boil over in a way that he would regret.

If Bill is to have a successful difficult conversation with Ann, he must find a way to express his anger toward her in a manner that is not blaming or judging. If he does take his frustration out on Ann, she will probably not hear anything constructive that he has to offer, and the problem will be compounded. The longer Bill carries his feelings around without talking to Ann, the harder it will be for him to be respectful.

How Do You Feel about Yourself in This Situation?

Any time you feel that your own worth or competence is in question, it will be very challenging for you to conduct yourself in a trustworthy manner in a difficult conversation. If you say to yourself—"I'm so stupid"; "I'm such a jerk"; "Who do you think you are, anyway"; "I'm an incompetent idiot"; "Nobody likes me"—or any variation on these themes, it's time to slow down and come to grips with yourself, because these are all indicators that your identity as a person has come into play. Other warning signs are feelings of shame, humiliation, worthlessness, or exposure, and feeling unlovable or unlikable.

There is a great tendency to blame such feelings of insufficiency on others: "It's your fault I feel this way!" The truth is that your sense of self-worth and competence is your responsibility and yours alone. No one can make you feel bad about yourself. It is true that if you already have a pocket of low self-esteem, others may say or do things that trigger an insufficiency reaction in you.

For the most part, conflictual situations have nothing to do with your identity. They are not an ultimate test of your worth as a person or your competence as an educator. There is nothing real hanging in the balance. Your feelings of inadequacy seek confirmation and seduce you into doing battle with ghosts. You project your lack of self-worth onto others and believe that they hold this lowly opinion of you.

You can make yourself into a more reliable person in conflict by building your sense of sufficiency. To feel better about yourself, act from your values, make your walk and your talk match, don't let your inner critic take charge, look to yourself for solutions, be respectful toward others, and have difficult conversations when they are needed.

As he thought about the situation with Ann, Bill saw that he was not feeling competent as the chairman of the committee. This was his first attempt at chairing a group, and he had no experience in leading difficult people. Everytime Ann spoke, Bill realized that he felt like a failure. He feared that he did not have what it takes to be a good leader. The more she talked, the smaller he felt.

Bill decided to take a different look at his leadership of the committee. He made a list of the things that he thought he had done well: sending out agendas and minutes promptly, asking thought-provoking questions, trying to elicit the ideas of each member, using humor to lighten up the discussion. The only negative he could think of was his failure to set boundaries for Ann. On balance, he decided that he was doing well in his first chairmanship. He also recognized that he should have been more proactive about Ann's participation, and he resolved to talk with her before the next meeting.

Once Bill became conscious that he had attached his own feelings of worth to Ann's behavior, he could set about dismantling this connection. He took his own inventory as a leader and made a realistic assessment of his current strengths and weaknesses. He made a plan for corrective action. Now when he has his difficult conversation with Ann, he won't be sidetracked by his own mistaken feelings of inadequacy.

What Impact Has the Other Person Had on You and on the Work of Your Group?

One of the greatest gifts you can give to a colleague is to give her specific feedback about the impact of her behavior. Without feedback, we are likely to continue on our way, wondering why we are not getting the results we want. Receiving accurate feedback is like getting a roadmap to help us get to where we want to go.

Bill determined that Ann was having a negative impact in three ways that she probably did not intend. She was slowing down the work of the group by continuing to repeat the same points. She was frustrating Bill as he tried to accomplish the tasks of the group in an efficient manner.

Perhaps most important of all, her ideas were lost as the group tuned out her excessive rhetoric.

Bill's precise understanding of Ann's impact on the committee will help him to intervene on her behavior. By giving her detailed feedback, he can offer her an opportunity to become a more effective member of the group.

What's Your Part in the Problem?

Problems are almost always co-created. If you think that the other person is solely to blame, it is time to look again. It is usually much easier to see the other person's part than it is to see your own contribution. You have to set aside your righteous indignation in order to frankly examine your portion of the dynamic.

Curiosity and open-mindedness will assist you in recognizing your own mistakes; harsh self-criticism will get in your way. As a human, you will make many mistakes. If you accept mistakes as an important part of the learning process, it is easier to admit to yourself that you have made them. It's how you handle those mistakes that will or will not build trust with others. Making the same mistake over and over without the self-responsibility of course correcting destroys trust.

> Bill recognized that his timidity in setting limits on Ann's excessive talking early in the committee process was his part of the problem. He had felt confused about how to handle this type of situation with a peer. His mentor could have helped him to grow into his new leadership role, but Bill had not thought to consult him. With this new insight, Bill scheduled an appointment with his mentor, who advised him on how to help bring Ann's ideas forward while limiting her speaking time.

When Bill began his preparation for a difficult conversation with Ann, he thought that the problem was all hers. By taking an honest look at the larger picture, he found his own contribution to the situation. Based on his insight, he created an opportunity to acquire new skills so that he would not make the same mistake in the future.

Who Have You Already Talked to about the Situation?

When you talk to a third party about a problem you have with someone else, you have usually created an unproductive triangle, which makes the situation more complex. The one exception is when you seek counsel from a mentor about how to alter your own behavior to create a breakthrough in the problem. Even consulting a mentor can contribute to the problem if you do it *instead* of having a difficult conversation.

> With an uneasy feeling in his stomach, Bill made a list of the people he had talked to about Ann's verbosity. He had commiserated with the committee members who had sought him out privately to complain about Ann. Bill had also griped about Ann to a teacher friend who was not on the committee. Because Bill placed high values on respect and on being a proactive part of solutions, he regretted the third-partying he had done about Ann.
>
> Bill also put his wife on the list. After each of the committee meetings, he had vented at length about Ann to his wife. Bill knew that this didn't create any problems at school, but saw that he should have recognized his repeated complaints as a warning signal that indicated the need to take action with Ann. Talking with his wife had left him just comfortable enough that he had not felt compelled to have the difficult conversation with Ann.

Bill accurately assessed that his talking to others about Ann, rather than speaking with her directly, was also part of his contribution to the problem. Acting against his values created an uncomfortable dissonance in Bill, which was a signal to him that he was out of integrity with regard to Ann.

What's the Worst Thing That Could Happen If You Had This Difficult Conversation?

It's helpful to get your fears out in the open. Exactly what do you feel you are risking? How likely are your fears to come true if you proceed? Often when you say your fears out loud, they sound absurd. If you leave your fears unnamed, they have power over you, sometimes enough to silence you.

> Bill felt nervous at the prospect of approaching Ann to have a difficult conversation about her participation on the committee. It took him a while to sort out what he feared. He wondered if Ann would get angry with him. Would she make a scene or cry? Would she stop liking him?
>
> Bill also felt anxious about the impact he might have on the committee. If Ann reacted badly, would she become hostile in the meetings and take up even more time? This was the possible negative outcome that Bill feared the most.
>
> Bill thought about everything he knew about Ann from working with her for five years. He had never seen Ann get angry and take it out on anyone, even when she had strong feelings. "Besides," Bill thought ruefully, "I could probably survive if she did get angry." Bill decided that his worst fears were not so likely to occur and that it was worth the risk.

By naming his fears, Bill was able to take realistic stock of them. Now that he had evaluated his anxieties in the light of reality, he would not have to be burdened with them in his difficult conversation with Ann.

What Are the Possible Consequences of Not Having This Conversation?

As a counterbalance to your fears about having a difficult conversation, it is instructive to think of what might be the impact of remaining silent. What will it do to you? To your relationship with the other person? To your work group? Are you willing to pay the price?

> Bill was already feeling stressed about the situation with Ann, and he had spent a couple of sleepless nights worrying about it. He had a sense that his stress would continue and worsen if he remained silent.
>
> Bill was already feeling a rift in his working relationship with Ann. The whole point of the committee was to get special and regular classroom teachers to work better together.

His problem with Ann had the potential to deepen the rift between the groups.

Bill was also aware of the frustration felt by the other committee members about being held hostage by Ann's filibusters. There was the potential for people to drop out of the committee if the situation didn't change. He was also concerned that the important work of the committee might not be accomplished if things continued as they were.

Bill was no longer willing to shoulder his frustrations with Ann. He had a sense that he would feel less stressed if he talked with her. Bill saw that his conflict with Ann mirrored the struggles that the two sets of teachers were having with each other. He was afraid that it would impede the work of the group. Bill also didn't want to lose any of his committee members. He became aware that the consequences of not having the conversation with Ann far outweighed the possible negatives.

What Would It Take to Resolve This Situation to Your Satisfaction?

What do you want from the other person? Understanding what the problem is and knowing what you want as a remedy are two different things. To have a successful difficult conversation, you need to be clear on what you would like the outcome to be and then remain flexible about how it unfolds. Together, you may come up with a solution that you could not have imagined on your own.

Bill was clear that he wanted Ann to put forth her ideas in less time so that the process of the committee would be shorter, smoother, and more effective. He also wanted to retain all of the committee members, including Ann. In addition, Bill wanted all of the members of the committee to be more forthcoming with each other rather than resorting to confusing nonverbal cues.

To accomplish these objectives, Bill realized that he needed to do two things. First, he needed to have a respectful, private difficult conversation with Ann. Next, he needed to work with the whole committee to establish guidelines about how they would interact with each other in the future.

Bill's original goal was to stop Ann from talking so much. As he worked through the process of preparing for a difficult conversation, his objective expanded to improving communications among all of the members.

How Can You Walk Away from the Conversation with a Feeling of Success?

If your definition of success for your difficult conversation is getting your way, you are setting yourself up for failure. If you are trying to get your way, you will probably wind up being controlling, which is never conducive to creative problem solving.

Another slippery slope to avoid is the need to have the other person change in order to feel successful. The only person you can change is yourself, and the same is true for the other person. It is important that your definition of success for the interaction relates to something over which you actually have control. Otherwise, you will be at the mercy of the other person. What you do have control over is how you conduct yourself in the conversation.

> Although Bill dearly wished he could control Ann's talking, he realized that this was not something that was within his domain. So Bill decided that he could feel good about the difficult conversation if he told Ann the truth with specificity and kindness, acknowledged his own role in the problem, and really listened to what she had to say in return.

Bill's definition of success for the upcoming difficult conversation with Ann was limited to his own behavior. Nothing Ann could do or say could prevent him from feeling successful at the end of their talk.

What Do You Appreciate and Value about the Other Person?

In order to bring your compassion to the table in a difficult conversation, it helps to remind yourself of what you respect about the other person. If you can do this, it will help you to be present mentally, emotionally, and spiritually during the discussion.

In order to find a win/win solution, you first have to find some way to connect with each other. If there is no idea that you can both relate to at the beginning of your discussion, you will need to come together through your respect and regard for each other. It is possible to do this even if you have a general dislike for the other person. Very few people on the planet do not have some redeeming qualities.

> By the time he got to this final question in his preparation for having a difficult conversation with Ann, Bill could remember that there were things about Ann that he truly valued. He thought about the special help that she had given to one of his hearing-impaired students and the time she had been such a good sport in the dunking booth at the school carnival. The note that she sent him when his mother died also came to mind. These memories helped Bill to recall that he appreciated Ann's thoughtfulness, sense of humor, and willingness.

Bill's insights into what he values about Ann will help him to remember that he is dealing with a whole person when he meets with her, not just with someone who talks too much. His appreciation of Ann's good qualities will aid him in keeping from dealing with her too harshly. In the next chapter, we follow Bill through his difficult conversation with Ann.

Chapter Summary

Preparing yourself for a difficult conversation creates the opportunity for you to be clear and spontaneous when you actually talk with the other person. These are the questions that you need to think about before you initiate a courageous conversation:

- ♦ Specifically, what's bothering you?
- ♦ When and how did this situation begin?
- ♦ What is your source of information?

- What assumptions have you made about the other person?
- How do you feel about the other person and the situation?
- How do you feel about yourself in the situation?
- What impact has the other person had on you and on your work together?
- What's your part in the problem?
- Who have you already talked to about the situation?
- What's the worst thing that could happen if you had this conversation?
- What are the possible consequences of *not* having this conversation?
- What do you want from the other person in order to resolve the problem?
- How can you walk away from the conversation with a feeling of success?
- What do you appreciate and value about the other person?

Chapter 7

Having a Difficult Conversation

Once you have prepared yourself to have a difficult conversation, it is time to put your planning into action. You will need to invite the other person to talk with you and then sit down together to communicate. There is no magic formula for a successful difficult conversation; however, there are basics that will help you work together to achieve a better understanding of each other and the problem so that you can find a win/win solution together.

In this chapter, we continue to follow Bill, the teacher who chaired a committee of his peers to improve the effectiveness of special education and regular classroom teachers in working together to help students. In the last chapter, Bill prepared for a difficult conversation with Ann, another teacher on the committee.

Inviting the Other Person to Have a Conversation

When a courageous conversation is needed, it is most effective to have it as quickly as possible. That way the material will be fresh in both of your minds, you will reduce your stress level, and the speculation on both sides will not have time to develop a life of its own. It is an act of honor and respect to be honest with another person in a timely manner.

If you can say what you need to say on the spot and have a successful conversation, more power to you. It's also fine if you need to gather your thoughts before engaging the other person. The longest you should wait to initiate the conversation is one week. If you make this a consistent guideline for yourself, it will help you to find the courage you need to say what's on your mind. The more you risk speaking up, the easier it will become. Like any other set of skills, difficult conversations become easier and less scary with practice.

There are several elements that you need to include in your invitation to the other person with whom you wish to have a challenging conversation. You should give the other person an invitation to solve the problem with you; a brief statement of the topic you wish to cover in the conversation; and a suggested location for the conversation. You may also wish to share the format that you are using to prepare for the conversation. Let's look more deeply at each of these elements.

Invite the Other Person to Solve the Problem with You

Thinking of initiating a difficult conversation as an invitation to solve a problem together helps you to set a cooperative tone from the beginning. If you see your goal as working together to arrive at a mutually beneficial solution to a problem, you are less likely to be combative or blaming. The other person has an opportunity to feel the good will in your intention and is more likely to participate in an open, self-responsible way.

State the Problem Briefly As You Currently See It

If you let the other person know what you want to talk about, she has an opportunity to focus on the issue and to prepare for the conversation, too. If you do not let her know what the parameters of the discussion are, she may move into unproductive speculation about what caused you to ask for the conversation.

At worst, it could illicit paranoia in the other person, who will then be on the defensive from the outset of the conversation. If the other person lies awake at night wondering what she has or hasn't done to displease you, the stage will not be set for successful communication between you.

The statement of the problem is a reflection of your current views. You may find that at the end of your successful difficult conversation your ideas about the situation have changed. It is important to enter the exchange with an open mind about your position. If you do not, you are likely to try to control the interaction, which will not be conducive to finding a win/win solution. The goal is a mutually satisfying resolution, not getting your own way.

Suggest a Time and Location for the Conversation

The two important aspects of location for the conversation are privacy and neutrality. Pick a place where other people will not disturb you. People walking in on your conversation or phoning you will disrupt the flow of your interaction. Be prepared to turn off your cell phone or your pager while you talk. Furthermore, this conversation is the business only of you and the other person. Try to schedule it for a place that is private enough not to ignite conjecture on the part of others.

The conversation should not be held in either of your offices or classrooms. Pick a neutral place to talk. We tend to get more territorial in our own spaces, and you may feel at somewhat of a disadvantage on the other person's turf. Finding common ground is a good metaphor for what you want to occur in the conversation.

If You Choose, Share the Format That You Are Using to Prepare for the Conversation

If you are using the questions in Chapter 7 of this book to prepare for the conversation, you may or may not wish to share them with the other person in your invitation. There is no right answer about whether to do this or not.

If you do decide to share the preparation questions with the other person, it is essential that you do so as a peer, not as a teacher. It would be appropriate to give the questions as courteous information about your process, not as an instruction about how to do it right. The latter approach would put you in a one-up position, which would not be conducive to mutual problem solving.

If you want to give the other person the opportunity to prepare in the same way that you are getting ready for the conversation, you might say, "To prepare for our conversation, I've been working with a set a questions I discovered in a book. If you'd like, I'll give you a copy of the questions." This does not put pressure on the other person; it simply provides her with information.

Bill Invites Ann to Have a Difficult Conversation

After Bill used the questions in Chapter 7 to prepare for a difficult conversation with Ann, he found a moment to approach her privately after school. He said, "Ann, I'd like your help in resolving a problem that I see. I don't think that our committee to improve communication between special ed and classroom teachers is operating as effectively as possible. I think that you are talking a great deal about your ideas and not really being heard by the group." Ann nodded and said, "I agree, and it doesn't feel very good."

Bill continued, "I'd like your help in remedying that situation. Would you be willing to meet with me tomorrow right after school in the library conference room to talk about it? I don't think we'll be disturbed there."

Ann replied, "I can't do it tomorrow because of soccer practice, but I could do it the next day. Would that be okay?"

"Yes." Bill said, "That would be good for me, too. I appreciate your willingness to work with me on this."

Bill successfully included all of the elements of an effective invitation to have a difficult conversation. He invited Ann to work with him to resolve a problem, which he briefly outlined. He found out that Ann saw the problem, too. He negotiated a specific place and time for a private conversation. The tone of his communication to Ann was respectful and collegial. As a result, they are off to a promising start.

The Courageous Conversation

What follows is a discussion of the parts of a successful difficult conversation. Do not plan on following this as a step-by-step outline for how to conduct the conversation. Rather, by the end of the conversation, try to incorporate all of the elements. If you let the conversation flow naturally and then double check to make sure that you have covered everything, you will have a more productive meeting.

You will begin by talking about the problem as you currently see it. Throughout, you will engage in deep listening to the other person's point of view. You will make sure that both of you state and clarify your assumptions about each other and the process. Both of you will ask for what you want, and you will work together to find a creative win/win solution. Now, let's take a more detailed look at each of the elements of a successful difficult conversation.

Lay Out Your Current View of the Problem

When you have initiated a courageous conversation, it is up to you to start it off. You may want to begin by setting a context for the problem and clarifying your intentions for the conversation. In presenting your current view of the problem, it is important to be as specific as possible and to present the information in a nonjudgmental manner. You also will want to provide the other person with feedback about the impact of his or her behavior, in addition to owning your own part in the problem.

Set the context, and clarify your intentions for the conversation. If this conversation is taking place in a larger context, identify how it fits together. It will help the other person to feel more at ease if you let her know clearly what your intentions are for the conversation.

Be specific and nonjudgmental. Talking in generalities is not productive. If Bill were to say to Ann, "You are rude in meetings," he would not be giving her any useful information; he would merely be judging her. Providing examples will help the other person to understand your view of the problem. If the behavior that you are questioning seems out of character for the other person, let her know.

Provide feedback about the other person's impact on your work together. If you believe that the other person's behavior has obstructed the accomplishment of workplace tasks, let her know. Clarify what the other person's intentions have been with regard to getting the work done. Don't just assume that her impact and her intentions match.

Provide feedback about the impact of the other person's behavior on your work relationship. Let the other person know how you are feeling about her behavior, without blaming her for your feelings. Acknowledge the importance of your work relationship. Remember, you do not have to like the other person in order to respect the fact that it is important for you to be able to work and communicate well together to accomplish the goals of your workplace.

Own your own part in the problem. There is nothing more disarming than taking responsibility for your role in a problem. To do so is an invitation to mutual problem solving and to letting the other person know that you are not blaming her for the whole situation. State it simply and apologize. Don't engage in self-flagellation; beating yourself up is never constructive, and it keeps you from thinking clearly.

Although you have several points to cover, it is essential to be brief in your first comments. If you take more than a couple of minutes the first time you speak, the other person may begin to glaze over from too much input. You can always expand on your ideas later in the conversation.

Listen Carefully to the Other Person's View of the Problem

You may think that you have a clear idea of what the other person's response will be to your view of the problem. It is important to hold lightly to that view so that you can listen carefully to her actual response.

When you initiate a difficult conversation, you have the opportunity to collect your thoughts and prepare yourself emotionally ahead of time. The other person may or may not come to the conversation with the same level of preparation. Try to let the other person talk without interrupting so that she can gather her thoughts. You may need to listen to her flounder through the kind of thinking that you got to do in private. Don't latch onto her first reaction—let her have space to explore the issues aloud.

Remain Curious about the Way the Other Person Sees Things

Even if you don't like the initial positions taken by the other person, it is important to remain curious and try to understand her point of view. There is an internal logic to most people's thinking. It will help you to work with the other person if you can understand the way she thinks about the problem. If you both saw the issues the same way in the first place, you probably wouldn't need to have a difficult conversation.

Staying curious requires that you suspend judgment about the other person and her intentions. You are not looking for ammunition to support your own point of view or to prove that you are right and she is wrong. If you maintain your curiosity, you will be able to achieve a much deeper understanding of the situation. Without curiosity, you will lose your compassion for the other person and will be more likely to have a fight, rather than a productive difficult conversation.

Ask Clarifying Questions

If you don't understand what the other person is talking about, ask her for clarification. Do not try to fill in the blanks by yourself. You will just be guessing and are likely to get it wrong. The questions you ask may also be helpful to the other person as she seeks to unscramble her own reactions. A perceptive question can cut right to the heart of a problem.

Once you believe you understand what the other person has said, check to make sure that you are correct. Restate what you think you heard in your own words, and ask her if that is what she meant. If she says that is not what she intended, then listen again, ask more clarifying questions, restate what you think she's telling you, and check with her again about your perceptions. You may have to repeat this several times before the two of you achieve clarity.

It is worth the time and energy to be completely clear with each other. If you walk away from the conversation with two different impressions of what has transpired, you will only compound the problem and further erode the trust between you.

Find Out about the Other Person's Intentions

Going into the conversation, you know the impact that the other person's behavior has had on you, but you do not know what her intentions were. To assume that you know what her intentions were would be an act of arrogance. It is appropriate and constructive to ask her about her intentions.

You can ask about the other person's intentions with an open-ended request: "It would help me to understand this situation better if you would tell me what your intentions were." Alternatively, you can ask a more specific question: "It seemed like you were intending to undermine my authority, but I'm not sure I'm right about that. Was that your intention?"

When people trade accusations about their intentions, the conversation is likely to fail. Giving feedback to each other about impact is useful information, especially when both of you also clarify your intentions toward each other. You know the intentions you have had toward the other person, but you will not know the actual impact of your behavior on her unless she tells you.

Check and Clarify Your Assumptions about Each Other

Some of the most serious conflicts are generated by the assumptions we make about each other and don't check for accuracy.

We may make assumptions about each other's work and about our relationships with each other.

Our silent assessments of someone else's work often lead to actions that will cause conflict and prevent us from seeing more constructive options.

- He's just putting in his time until he retires, so I won't ask him to be on the leadership team. (If you asked him, he might tell you that being on the leadership team would be a great way to spice up his last year of teaching.)

- I'd have to redo this when she finished, so I might as well just do it myself. (What if you gave her clear instructions and developed a plan together so she could actually be of help to you?)

- He's not very competent at teaching algebra, so I'm sure he wouldn't be any good at teaching geometry, either. (Geometry requires different teaching skills than algebra does—maybe he's misplaced in his current role, and a change could make all the difference.)

- She can't control her class, so I will make sure that I share the field trip bus with another teacher. (If the impact of her lack of student discipline is not addressed directly, she may inaccurately assume that you have a personality conflict with her.)

- If we share a classroom, he will leave it messy; I can't handle that, so I'll make up some excuse to get out of it. (If you talk about your style differences directly, it does not need to result in a conflict.)

Our clandestine assumptions about our relationships are often based on "evidence" we have collected. We don't stop to consider that the evidence may have an interpretation that does not reflect poorly on us.

- She's doesn't like me. I can tell because she never responds when I say "hello" to her in the hall. (What if she is just in her own world and doesn't notice when people greet her.)

- He doesn't really want to team teach with me next year; otherwise, he would have talked to me about it by now. (He could be thinking the same thing about your silence.)
- She doesn't trust me to speak for myself; that's why she always completes my sentences for me. (Perhaps she has a bad habit that has nothing to do with her opinion of you).
- She didn't look at me during my presentation. I know she hated it. (She might be completely absorbed in a problem about which you are unaware.)

Before you finish your difficult conversation, make sure that you each have an opportunity to check out your unspoken assessments of each other. If you don't, they will reemerge in another conflict.

Find Out What Each of You Wants to Consider the Problem Solved

Your request for a solution to the problem should be specific so that you will know when the issue has been successfully laid to rest. Here are some examples:

- I want you to make a commitment to be on time to school every day.
- If I tell you something in confidence, I want to know that I can count on you to keep it to yourself.
- If you have a problem with something I have done, I want you to tell me directly, rather than going to the superintendent to complain about me.
- I don't want you to shout at me when we disagree.
- I'd like for you to limit the time you complain in my presence to five minutes a day so that I can be present for your concerns and so that I won't feel overdosed on negativity.

Determine whether the other person is able and willing to do what you request. If not, work with the other person to come up with another alternative. What you are looking for is not a compromise, where both of you give in on what you really want. Instead, you are seeking a new, creative approach that will genuinely work for both of you.

Take the time to find a win/win solution. An excellent solution is one that will leave you both feeling better about yourselves and will create the conditions for a more productive working relationship. If you reach an impasse, schedule a second conversation and commit to returning with new possibilities. Delayed processors may need to go away and think in order to generate further options.

Take Action to Implement Your Plan

Once you have agreed upon a course of corrective action with the other person, it is important that you both keep your part of the bargain. Having a successful difficult conversation is the first step in restoring trust between you. The second step is to keep your word and do your part to follow up on your conversation.

Wait awhile to let your new agreements manifest, and then check in with the other person to confer on how you both think it is going. If your solutions have proved inadequate, or if you are not sticking to your agreements, you need to retool your plan.

Bill and Ann's Difficult Conversation

When Bill and Ann met in the library conference room after work, Bill closed the door and said, "I'm going to turn off my cell phone so we won't be disturbed. This conversation is important to me, and I want to give it my full attention."

"Thank you for agreeing to meet with me. I think that our task together on the committee to improve the working relationships between our two groups of teachers is important. I think everyone suffers when we don't have our act together—the students, the regular classroom teachers, and the special ed staff."

"As the chairperson of the committee, I feel responsible for how the committee works together. I'm concerned that we don't seem to be communicating very well. I'd like your help in improving how we interact."

"I've noticed that you talk a great deal on this committee. In fact, I've observed that you talk about as much as all of the other members combined. I believe that you have good ideas, and you repeat them over and over. For example, in the last meeting, you told us that story about your student who missed the prep session for the science test because he had to leave for speech therapy. That was the fourth time you had told us that story, and it didn't help to hear it again."

"As I see it, the impact of all your verbiage is that the rest of us tune you out and don't pay attention to your ideas. I don't want your ideas to be lost. Also, the work of the committee is taking way too long. People don't mind serving on a committee if they believe in the task and if accomplishing it takes a reasonable amount of time. I'm worried that we will lose committee members because the work is taking too much time."

"The impact on me is that I feel frustrated with you. I feel as though you are holding the committee hostage, and I don't understand why. I feel that our lack of progress reflects badly on my leadership ability. You and I have worked together successfully for years. We have accomplished a great deal together, and I value our working relationship. I have never before experienced you as dominating the conversation in a group. I'm curious about what is different about this situation."

"I know that I share a part in this problem. I was short with you in the last meeting. I apologize for saying "Are you finished?" in such a rude way. If I had spoken to you when I first started to feel frustrated, I wouldn't have taken a sideswipe at you like that."

"Thank you for hearing me out, Ann. Now I'd like to hear your thoughts on the situation."

Ann, who had been holding her breath, let out a deep sigh. "Wow! I had no idea that I was being such a bigmouth. I hate it when people talk too much. Even though I'm embarrassed to learn that I've been doing it, I'm really glad that you told me."

"Actually, it may explain something that's been irritating me. I've noticed in the last couple of meetings that some of the special ed teachers on the committee have been looking away and rolling their eyes when I talk. I thought that they were disagreeing with my ideas, so I just tried harder to get them across. Now I wonder if they didn't just want me to stop talking so much."

"This has been the worst school year I've ever had, Bill. The budget cuts put five extra students in each of my classes, and I can't get the lab equipment I need. I have been feeling frantic. It seems like I can't get around to each student, and more and more students are falling behind. I have such high standards for my students and myself, and I'm not meeting them as I have in the past. I feel so frustrated, and there's nothing I can do about it."

"I think when any extra thing happens, it just pushes me over the edge. A good example is that story I've apparently been telling *ad nauseam* about my student who missed the test prep session for speech therapy. I can't keep up with what's happening when everything is going well, let alone when I have students coming and going from my classroom."

Bill interjected, "I had no idea you were feeling so overwhelmed, Ann. With the budget cuts, we've really taken a hit in special ed, too. It's good for me to stop and think about what the impact has been on all of you classroom teachers. Apparently, we have all brought our frustrations to the committee, but we haven't talked about them directly."

"Yes," Ann said. "Now that I'm talking about all this, I recognize that I've been feeling powerless over what is happening around me. I think I've been trying to compensate by controlling what goes on in our committee meetings. I just want any interruptions to my classes to go away. That must be pretty frustrating for the special ed teachers. I know that you all have been hit hard by the budget cuts, too. I'm sorry, Bill."

"I'm sorry, too, Ann. I don't want to make your life any harder as I work with special ed students, and I don't think that my colleagues want that either. I think that what's been going on with you and the other members is a reflection of the larger problem that our committee has been convened to solve."

"Another way that I have contributed to the problem is by not fully taking charge of the process. I have seen other members of the committee change the subject after you have spoken, roll their eyes at you, and be dismissive of you in other ways; and I haven't done anything about it. I don't want us to treat you or anyone else like that anymore."

"In preparing for our conversation, I realized that I had an assumption that you did not trust my leadership of the committee. Is that the case?"

Ann replied, "No, Bill, that is not the case. I think that you have been doing a great job of trying to keep us on track. It's not your fault that I have been oblivious. I've appreciated the agendas and your sense of humor. You and I have a positive history together, so I never thought you were not listening to me. I didn't even notice what you thought of as rudeness in the last meeting. It's the other special ed members that I have found so frustrating. It may be because I don't really know any of them."

"What do you think we should do now, Bill?"

Bill responded, "I'd like to approach this in several ways. First, I would like to get a commitment from you, Ann, to reduce your airtime in the committee."

"Consider it done," said Ann.

Bill continued, "I'd also like to bring our concerns to the next meeting of the committee. We could start by telling the other members about our own frustrations and then listen to their concerns. I would like for us to come to some new agreements with each other about how we interact."

Ann replied, "I like that idea. Part of what I have to say will be an apology for my behavior. I would also like it if we would all agree to speak up right away when something is bothering us, rather than being so indirect with each other.

That would also help us to shift the troublesome dynamics between our two staffs."

"It sounds like we have a plan," said Bill. "Let's check in with each other after the meeting to see if we think we are on track."

Bill approached Ann in a respectful, collegial manner. He began the conversation with his view of the problem. He described the specific behavior that he found frustrating without blaming or judging her and provided an example. Bill provided Ann with feedback about her impact on the committee and apologized for his own rudeness toward her.

Ann was disarmed by Bill's directness and self-responsibility. She had been oblivious to her own behavior, the causes, and the impact. By talking about it with Bill, she realized that she was taking out her frustrations about the budget cuts on the committee. She committed to limit her talkativeness, and they developed a plan to help bring the committee to a new standard of interaction. This was a successful difficult conversation because both Bill and Ann left feeling better about themselves and with a plan of action to improve the workings of the committee.

What to Do If the Conversation Does Not Go Well

Despite your best efforts, difficult conversations are not always successful—they do not always end with win/win solutions and improved working relationships. The conversation might feel more like an unproductive fight with both of you defending your positions, instead of an attempt to work together to solve a problem. You might find that the other person is defensive, argumentative, hurt, or unwilling to participate. So, what next?

First, when your emotions have cooled, take a look at your role in the difficult conversation. With an attitude of curiosity, evaluate yourself on the following aspects of communication:

- Was I honest and specific about what was bothering me? Did I provide examples?
- Was I able to avoid shaming, blaming, judging, and using inflammatory language?
- Did I listen to the other person with an open mind?
- Were the timing and setting right to have the difficult conversation?
- Did my nonverbal communication and tone of voice match my words?
- Did I take responsibility for both my intentions and my impact?
- Did I check my assumptions with the other person?
- Did I try to find mutually satisfactory solutions, or was I trying to be right or to win?

If you discover that you did not conduct yourself as you had intended in the conversation, acknowledge the discrepancy between what you intended and what you actually did, and ask the other person if you can try again.

Resist the temptation to turn to a third party and complain about your lack of success with the person with whom you are in conflict. Ask for coaching from one person, if you believe you need it, without asking the coach to take sides with you. The only legitimate role for a coach is to help you improve your skills.

If you believe that your part of the conversation was clean and clear, wait until you find another logical opening to have a difficult conversation with the person and try again. Ask for feedback about what worked and didn't work for the other person in the first attempt. Think of a different way to express your concerns—sometimes a person can hear and understand something expressed one way and not another. If you have tried three times to have a difficult conversation and have not been successful, you might consider suggesting a facilitator.

It is possible that no matter what you do, you may not be able to have a successful difficult conversation with the other person. If that is the case, resist the temptation to write the other person off or exclude her.

You may have to make a complex decision about whether you can work with someone who will not engage productively in difficult conversations with you. You may be able to let go of your concerns and just accept the situation as it is. If that is not possible, then consider whether you want to work less closely with the person or to continue to work with the person at all. It is important for you to be clear with yourself about what you are willing to live with and what you are not. It is not fair to do nothing and feel resentful or complain to others about the situation. To do so would form an unproductive triangle.

Chapter Summary

When you want to initiate a difficult conversation, invite the other person to meet with you to solve the problem together. Give a brief statement of the problem as you currently see it. Suggest a time and private location for the conversation on neutral turf.

As the initiator, it is your responsibility to begin the conversation. Lay out your current view of the problem. Describe the difficulty very specifically, providing examples, and take care to avoid blaming and judging. Provide feedback about the impact of the other person's behavior on you and on your work together. Own your own part of the problem and, if necessary, apologize. This part of the conversation should take no more than two minutes, and it will set the tone for the rest of your interaction.

After you have described the problem, listen to the other person. Let her think out loud, and give her a chance to have her own insights into the problem. Then ask clarifying questions to be sure you understand what she is saying. Try to stay curious and compassionate.

Ask for information about the other person's intentions and clarify your own. If appropriate, ask for feedback about your own impact. Unearth your assumptions about the other person and ask if they are correct. Invite her to do the same with you.

Ask for what you would like in order to solve the problem. Find out what the other person wants. Work together to find a creative solution that will leave you both feeling better about yourselves and will help you work together better.

Demonstrate your trustworthiness by keeping your part of the bargain. Check in with the other person at a later date to make sure the plan is working. Correct course, if necessary.

If the difficult conversation does not result in a win/win solution, stop and take stock of the situation. Evaluate your own role in the conversation—have you conducted yourself as you intended? If the other person is uncooperative, try again, and express your concerns in a different way. If all of your efforts do not result in a successful difficult conversation, reevaluate your working relationship to determine what you can tolerate and what you cannot allow to continue.

Chapter 8

Heads Up . . . Incoming!

Responding When Someone Else Initiates A Difficult Conversation

When you initiate a difficult conversation, you have some control over the timing and your own readiness to participate. When someone else initiates the conversation, you may not have the luxury of preparing yourself. You may need to have the conversation on the spot.

It can be particularly unsettling when someone approaches you with velocity, demanding to be heard. The other person may be angry and accusatory. Your first impulse may be to flee. It is important that you stand your ground and participate in the conversation without allowing the other person to be abusive to you.

What you can do ahead of time is learn the skills of responding to someone who is coming at you. These practices will help you in all of your workplace interactions and especially when you are surprised by an insistent ultimatum to talk.

Breathe Deeply

When you feel attacked, you have a tendency to stop breathing. As soon as you hold your breath, the oxygen flow to your brain stops, which makes it more difficult for you to think clearly. Remembering to breathe deeply will help you to keep your wits about you.

People in the assault mode tend to speak rapidly and move quickly. If you match the attacker's pace, it is more likely that the conflict will escalate. Try to slow the interaction down by breathing deeply and talking more slowly than the other person.

In addition, try not to match the other person's tone. Do not meet his angry tone with your own angry attitude. Do your best to remain charge neutral, neither excited nor suppressed. If you can manage that, you will give the other person an opportunity to behave more responsibly, too.

> The afternoon kindergarten class had just left her classroom when Rosa looked up to see John, the head custodian, headed down the hall toward her with a scowl on his face and a purposeful look in his eye. Rosa felt intimidated by John, who was twice her size. She had always experienced him as critical and demanding, with a short fuse.
>
> As John came nearer, Rosa started to perspire, and her hands began to shake. When she felt lightheaded, she realized she wasn't breathing. So she took several deep breaths and felt calmer by the time John reached her door.
>
> John spoke to Rosa rapidly, in an accusing tone of voice, while he pointed his finger in her face. "Rosa, you left those cardboard boxes down in the boiler room, didn't you. I know it was you, so don't deny it."
>
> Rosa stood up straight, looked John in the eye, and replied calmly and slowly, "Yes, John, I left some empty cardboard boxes in the boiler room. I hope that didn't create a problem for you."
>
> "Well," John said, more slowly, "You didn't break them down, and that's not my responsibility. I can't recycle them unless they're broken down. If I had to break down all the boxes you people use, it would take me all day."

"I'm sorry, John," replied Rosa, continuing in a calm manner. "I didn't realize that I was supposed to break them down. I'll come down right now and do it. Next time, I'll do it before I bring them to you."

"All right, that's more like it," John said and walked away.

Rosa did not match John's rapid speaking pace or his angry tone. As she breathed deeply and spoke slowly and directly to John, he began to calm down. Because she was thinking clearly, Rosa realized that she had made a mistake in not breaking down the boxes. She apologized and volunteered to correct her error immediately.

It's Not about Me. It's Not about Me. It's Not about Me.

When the other person is angry and accusatory, it is easy to get caught in the trap of taking it personally. You believe that if you do not defend yourself, it will mean that you are a bad person, a loser, or an incompetent. When you feel like that, it means that your identity is engaged. You have been fooled into believing that this is a defining moment for you as a person or as a professional.

In reality, when someone is shaming, judging, or blaming you, it is a reflection of that person's character, not a statement about you. If the other person is in a reactive mode, he may think that it's all about you, but you do not have to buy into his perception.

It may turn out that you have actually made a mistake. This has nothing to do with the kind of person you are or whether you are a worthy professional. Everyone makes mistakes, sometimes big ones. You will be able to take suitable, timely and corrective action if you do not let yourself believe that your identity is threatened.

Furthermore, not personalizing an attack will protect you from perceiving yourself as a victim. Once you move into victim response mode, you will feel powerless and are likely to engage in unproductive behavior yourself. As a victim, you might let the other person treat you in an inappropriate way or you might feel entitled to strike back. Neither of these responses will lead to a productive conclusion. No matter how poorly the difficult conversation is initiated, your goal should still be to find a win/win solution.

Stay Curious and Listen Carefully

The best way to prevent becoming reactive is to stay curious. You may not like the way someone approaches you for a difficult conversation, but if you can manage to stay curious, you might learn something important and help to solve a problem. Look past the presentation for the opportunities for clarification and connection with the other person. Being actively curious—wanting to find out what's really happening—also helps you to avoid taking things personally or becoming self-critical.

Listen very carefully to all of what the other person is saying. Among the attack and the criticism, you may find a valid point. Ask questions to be sure that you understand what the other person is saying. If you have assumptions, check them out with the other person to be sure they are accurate.

Alan Alda has said that both acting and being the host of the PBS show *Nova* require deep listening. Alda elaborated,

> Listening doesn't take place unless you are willing to be changed by the person you're listening to. When you're not just waiting for a pause so you can say your thing, you're actually letting them have an effect on you. Where in you is my solution? Even if I think you sound like a nut, where is what you're saying going to change me and give me something I don't have already? If I'm listening like that, I'll come up with something I didn't expect.

That is the kind of listening that is required to have a successful difficult conversation.

Robert was surprised to find the mother of one of his students calling him at home on Friday night while he and his wife were entertaining friends. She launched right in, "Mr. Franklin and I are very worried about our Jackie. You are stressing her out! You're putting too much pressure on her with all that homework! Four hours of homework a night is too much for a fourth grader! She's up in her room all the time, and we never see her. I want to know what you're going to do about it."

As Jackie's mother talked, Robert was tempted to believe that he had done something wrong and that he was not a very good teacher. Fortunately, he recognized these thoughts as victim thinking and decided not to indulge in them. He replied, "Mrs. Franklin, I know that you care very much about Jackie and are concerned about her welfare. I care about her, too. I also agree with you that four hours a day of homework would be way too much for fourth graders. That's why I never assign more than an hour of homework a night."

Mrs. Franklin responded, "Well if she's not doing homework, what is she doing up there in her room?"

"That's a good question," replied Robert. "Jackie doesn't seem to be having difficulty with her schoolwork, so I can't explain why she would be spending so much extra time on her studies. I'd like to sit down together with you and Jackie and see if we can't get to the bottom of this. Can you come in on Monday?"

"I surely will be there. I wonder what that girl is up to. Thank you, Mr. Griffin. I'm sorry to have disturbed you on a Friday night."

Robert could easily have taken Mrs. Franklin's accusations personally. Because he didn't try to defend his identity as a good teacher, he was able to listen to her carefully and calmly give her the facts. Robert was curious about what was really going on with Jackie and her parents. He didn't attempt to speculate on what Jackie was actually doing when she claimed to be studying. Instead, he stuck to what he actually knew to be true. It was enough to defuse Mrs. Franklin.

Robert also deferred the rest of the conversation to a more appropriate time and place—the following Monday at school.

Had Mrs. Franklin attempted to continue the conversation on the phone, Robert would probably have needed to set a limit with her, saying, "I do want to talk with you and Jackie about this problem, but I cannot continue the conversation right now—my dinner guests are waiting for me."

Including Jackie in the conversation was the only way to resolve the issue. Having her parents and her teacher in the same room with her will help to elicit the missing information from Jackie. It is possible that Jackie was trying to present herself as a victim of Mr. Griffin and his excessive homework policies and that Mrs. Franklin assumed the role of rescuer. If an unproductive triangle has formed between Jackie, her parents, and Dan Griffin, they will only be able to effectively dismantle it if all of the parties are present.

If You're Feeling Highly Reactive, Ask for Time

When someone comes to you with a criticism or complaint, you may feel so angry or hurt that you can't think clearly. Unless the situation is an emergency that demands immediate attention, it is perfectly acceptable to ask to have the conversation at a later date.

If you do ask for time, it is important that you name a specific time when you will come back to have the conversation. Ideally, it should be no longer than 24 hours later. By asking for time to collect yourself, you are taking responsibility for your own reactivity, rather than projecting your feelings onto the other person. Other people's behavior may be a catalyst for your emotions, but you, and you alone, are responsible for how you act on those feelings.

Nancy had a particularly challenging fifth grade class. Many of the boys exhibited emotional problems and tended to express their problems through aggression or physical violence. At the end of each school day, she felt more tired than she had in previous school years.

Over the year, Nancy felt that she had made progress with her class because there were far fewer fights and major disruptions. One day in March, Nancy was walking her class to the gym for their play period. The boys in her line were playfully bopping each other on the head and laughing when they passed a line of second graders coming from the cafeteria with their teacher, Jill.

After school that day, Jill came to Nancy's room and said, "Your class's behavior is atrocious. You just let your children hit each other and did nothing about it. My little ones were watching all that hitting. Of course they look up to the fifth graders. When we got back to our classroom, my boys started hitting each other in the head and thought it was funny. I had a very hard time getting them to calm down and quit hitting each other. They think it's okay, because you let the big kids get away with it. This all happened because you can't control your class."

Nancy felt furious and defensive. She knew that if she tried to discuss the situation with Jill, she would explode and make things worse. So Nancy said to Jill, "I will have a conversation with you about this, but right now I'm so angry about the way you are talking to me that I couldn't be reliable. I should be able to think clearly about this by tomorrow. I'll come to your room after school if that's all right."

Jill replied, "Okay, but I don't know why you're so angry; I'm the one that had the problem."

Through gritted teeth, Nancy managed to say, "Thank you, I'll see you tomorrow."

Jill presented her concerns to Nancy in an attacking manner. Instead of sticking to her concerns about this specific incident, Jill globalized her accusations to include all of the behavior of Nancy's students and her general ability to keep discipline. Not surprisingly, Nancy was angered by Jill's words and tone.

Even through her fog of anger, Nancy suspected that Jill might have a legitimate point. Nancy knew that younger students imitate older students. Nancy's mind was racing with all of the rude things that she wanted to say to Jill. In order to avoid a catfight with Jill, Nancy knew that she had to go away and cool off before attempting to discuss the problem with Jill. Somehow, Nancy even managed to avoid sniping back when Jill delivered her parting shot.

That evening, as Nancy thought about her class's behavior in the hall, she realized that she had been so grateful that the boys were being playful with each other, instead of fighting, that she had failed to set appropriate limits with them. Part of why she had been so angry with Jill was that she knew there was truth in the complaint. The other part was that she didn't like the way Jill had talked to her about her concerns.

The next day, Nancy went to Jill's room right after school. Jill's greeting was, "Well, I didn't think you'd actually show up."

Nancy replied, "I am ready to talk with you now. I think you have a point about the impact of my students' behavior on your students. I don't want it to happen again. I want to work this out with you, and I don't like the way you talked to me about it yesterday or the way you greeted me today. I want you to stop being sarcastic and blaming so that we can work together to resolve this issue. This was one unfortunate incident—my whole ability to keep order with my students is not in question here."

Jill said, "You're right, Nancy. I'm sorry. Can we start over?"

Nancy built trust by keeping her commitment to reenter the difficult conversation with Jill. Nancy took responsibility for her part of the conflict and set appropriate limits on Jill's behavior toward her. Now they have a chance to have a successful difficult conversation.

Work to Preserve the Relationship

Regardless of how badly the other person is behaving or how deeply your disagreements run, you are probably going to have to continue working together. You can't divorce an insufferable colleague or an odious parent. As long as you are in your current role, you are stuck with each other. So you need to be able to communicate productively.

When you are faced with an angry or shaming person, focus on finding a way to preserve your working relationship. Let the other person know that it is important to you to be able to function together to achieve what you believe is important. Make it clear that you respect him or her as a member of the educational community. If you have successfully managed your reactivity, nothing can keep you from treating the other person respectfully.

Manuel, a human resources director, was working at his desk when his secretary came in and shut the door. "There's a very angry teacher out there. It's Stuart Smith from the high school," she said, sounding very nervous.

"It's okay, I know Stuart. I'll handle it," Manuel said and went out to speak with the teacher.

"Stuart," said Manuel, "Please come into my office and have a seat. You look pretty steamed; what's up?"

Stuart started in: "I have given my whole life to this school district. I have had enough money deducted from my paycheck to retire in Florida, and what do I have to show for it? My wife has cancer, and our so-called health benefits won't cover the only experimental treatment that might save her."

"How can you sit here in this cushy office, drawing a big salary, and live with yourself when you are screwing the rest of us out of the means to keep our families alive? If you didn't drive that big SUV, maybe we could get decent benefits."

Manuel responded, "Stuart, I'm so sorry to hear that your wife has cancer. That must be very frightening for both of you. Even a great teacher like you must find it hard to come to school every day and be faced with all those demanding teenagers. How are your own kids doing with their mom having cancer?"

Tears began to roll down Stuart's face as he said, "They're scared to death and so am I. I love Margie so much. I don't know what I would do without her. I don't know how I could be both a mom and a dad to my own teenagers. They need me to be strong right now, so I'm trying not to let them know how I feel. I don't think it's working. I feel like I'm failing everywhere. I can't make Margie well, I can't be a strong enough father, and I'm just going through the motions at school." Stuart began to sob, and Manuel sat quietly with him and let him cry.

"I'm sorry, Manuel. I'm sorry for crying and for yelling at you. I didn't mean all that stuff I said. I know you work hard for your money, just like the rest of us. These days I get stupid angry—my brain flies out the window, and my mouth keeps going."

Manuel responded, "I know it was just the grief talking, Stuart. I don't know what I would do if my wife had cancer. I want so much to help you and your family."

"There are a couple of things I can think of right away. First, if you give me information about your wife's condition and the treatment that might work for her, I will contact the insurance company and see what I can do. Sometimes, I have had success in getting them to bend their coverage policies."

"Second, I know that our employee assistance program has services for families who are going through a health crisis. You and your children deserve skilled professional help to get through this. Anyone would."

"Thank you, Manuel. Thank you for your offers of help. I'm going to take you up on both of them. Most of all, thank you for listening, even when I was a jerk."

"I'm so glad you came in today, Stuart. I'll do everything in my power to assist."

In the face of Stuart's attack, Manuel could easily have responded in kind or refused to continue the conversation. Instead, Manuel ignored the personal accusations and kept listening. Manuel also took the opportunity to acknowledge his respect for Stuart as a good teacher. By both the content and tone of his response, Manuel preserved his working relationship with Stuart. Manuel honored his connection with Stuart and Stuart's emotional state before moving on to the task of helping Stuart solve his problems.

More than anything else, Stuart needed a compassionate response, and he got it. Manuel gave Stuart the opportunity to acknowledge and take responsibility for his own inappropriate behavior.

Manuel was especially wise in allowing Stuart to cry uninterrupted. If Manuel had spoken or offered a box of tissues, Stuart's healing experience of crying with another, caring human being might have ended prematurely. There was nothing legitimately reassuring that Manuel could have said to Stuart. It's fine to offer tissues when someone finishes crying or asks for them. Often, efforts to interrupt in some way when another person is crying are the result of the discomfort of the listener, disguised to look like a helpful intervention.

Acknowledge the Impact of Your Actions and Apologize

If you have done something that has hurt another person in some way, whether you intended the harm or not, you have had a negative impact. If you rush to defend yourself by stating what your intentions were before you acknowledge the negative impact that you had, you will only enrage the other person.

Start by taking responsibility for the fallout from your actions and apologize. If you need to make amends in some way, arrange to do so. Then you can say what your intentions were. If they were not honorable to start with, own up to that fact. For example, you might say, "I was very angry, and I wanted to hurt you."

If your impact was different from what you intended, let the other person know. Usually, when we have had a negative impact, we did not intend to do harm to the other person.

If you have actually harmed someone in any way, an apology seems natural. When you cannot perceive harm to the other person and feel misunderstood yourself, it may be harder to think about offering an apology. You may even be faced with someone demanding an apology that you think is unwarranted.

An excellent reason to apologize, whether you think you have caused injury or not, is to preserve your working relationship with the other person. You never need to apologize for something you did not do, but you can always find something that is a legitimate apology.

If all else fails, you can say, "I'm sorry, I would never want to have a negative impact on you." This is not admitting that you did anything wrong, merely that the working relationship is important enough to you that you would not want to be the source of anything damaging. If someone asks for an apology, give it. You can only pull this off if you are not reactive.

Yi Min was the gifted and talented coordinator for her school district. An angry parent stormed into her office without an appointment. "I'm Joe Thomas, Matt's father. We got a letter from you telling us that Matt didn't get into the gifted program because," . . . he continued, reading from the letter, "'Matt has not continued to exhibit exceptional performance beyond what can be handled in the regular classroom.'"

"How dare you say that my Matt isn't smart? He beats me at chess almost every night. Now what average kid can do that? What prestigious college will accept a kid who looks average? You're blowing my boy's future."

"And another thing—in my company, all of the other managers' children are in gifted and talented programs in their schools. How do you think it makes me feel to have Matt in just a 'regular' classroom?"

Yi Min, who did not believe that any real harm had been done to Matt by not admitting him to the gifted and talented program, paused and then spoke, "Mr. Thomas, I apologize. I would never want to harm Matt or cause him difficulties later in his life. Nor would I want to cause you any embarrassment. Will you sit down and talk with me about Matt?"

"Humph," grunted Mr. Thomas as he sat down.

Yi Min continued, "Matt is a very smart boy. Unfortunately, the district only has the funds for one percent of our students to participate in the gifted and talented program. Matt is in the top five percent, but not the top one percent. I wish we had the resources to serve the top ten percent. Matt's not being selected for the gifted and talented program is not a poor reflection on him, merely the reality of the state of funding for education. That's something that you can tell your colleagues."

"I can also assure you that seventy percent of our students go on to university. Usually, the top ten percent have no difficulty in getting admitted to the top schools, provided they keep up their grades and participate in extracurricular activities. I would be happy to meet with you and Matt to discuss ways that you can work as a family to enrich his educational experience and prepare him to apply for college."

"Hmm," Mr. Thomas replied. "It's not what I wanted, but maybe this isn't as big a disaster as I thought."

Yi Min could hear that Mr. Thomas was feeling embarrassed by his son's not being admitted to the gifted and talented program. He had the false impression that it reflected poorly on Matt's intelligence. Without realizing it, he had personalized the district's budget constraints.

Yi Min led with an apology, even though she could see no harm to either the father or the son. She let Mr. Thomas know that she did not want to have a negative impact on his family and that she cared about his feelings and the effect she had on his son. Her apology helped Mr. Thomas to listen to what she had to say about the realities of the gifted and talented program. She provided factual, reassuring information. Her offer to provide further assistance to the family was generous and disarming.

What Would You Like Me to Do?

Find out what the other person wants you to do. If an angry person has an unspoken request, she will only become more outraged if that expectation is not met. If the person does not know what she wants, she may never feel satisfied, no matter what you do.

When someone is upset and approaches you with velocity, often she does not really know what she wants as an outcome. Alternatively, she may come in asking for one thing and, in the course of the conversation, realize that she really wants something else.

Your role is to keep asking for clarification until you are both certain that you understand what the other person wants. More often than not, the other person just wants to be heard. You may not need to do anything but listen; however, it is important that you both come to a clear understanding.

If the other person does make a clear request for you to do something, then you have to determine whether you are willing and able to do what is being asked. If you will not or cannot meet the request, it is most helpful to suggest several alternative solutions. You will need to be creative together to find something that works for both of you.

Mr. Brooks, an elementary principal, was supervising students as they boarded their school buses to go home when an angry parent accosted him. Mrs. Watkins shouted, "Mr. Brooks, what kind of school are you running up here? My son Jamal is being bullied, and I don't like it!"

Mr. Brooks responded calmly, "Mrs. Watkins, I want to give you my full attention to talk about your concerns. I need to finish loading the children onto their buses before we talk. I know you want all of the little ones to be safe. Would you go on in and wait for me in my office. I'll be with you in just a few minutes."

"I'll be waiting," Mrs. Watkins snapped.

True to his word, Mr. Brooks didn't keep Mrs. Watkins waiting long. He entered his office and said, "I appreciate your waiting for me, Mrs. Watkins. Now, I'd like to hear what you have to say about Jamal."

Mrs. Watkins sniffed, "That boy Tony in Jamal's third-grade class keeps roughing up Jamal on the playground and calling him names. Jamal is small for his age and very sensitive. I don't want him being called 'sissy' and pushed and shoved. Jamal is scared, and he doesn't know how to deal with it. Every morning he pleads with me not to make him go to school. This, from a straight A student!"

Mr. Brooks responded, "I don't want Jamal or any other student in this school to be bullied. Do you know where this is taking place? Does their teacher know about it?"

"Jamal says it happens on the playground every day at recess, when the supervisors aren't looking," said Mrs. Watkins. "He doesn't want to tell on Tony because he thinks that's cowardly. I'm a single parent, and I don't know how to teach a boy to defend himself. Besides, I don't want him to become a fighter."

Mr. Brooks said, "I can see you've given this situation a good deal of thought, Mrs. Watkins. Is there something in particular that you'd like for me to do?"

"Yes, there is," she said. "I want you to take Tony out of Jamal's class and put him in some other class that doesn't have recess or lunch or anything else with Jamal. That way, Jamal won't have to deal with him, and he won't be scared to come to school."

"That's an interesting idea, and I'm not sure it would be fair to either Jamal or Tony," he said.

"What do you mean?" she inquired.

"Both boys have something important to learn. Jamal needs to learn how to stand up for himself without retaliating in kind. He will likely face other bullies in his life, and it will be good for him to develop confidence in handling them at this early age. As for Tony, he needs to learn how to stop being a bully and learn to connect with others in a more positive way. The earlier we can intervene on a bully, the more likely we are to create a permanent behavior change."

"Here's what I propose to do," Mr. Brooks continued. "For starters, now that I know when and where the bullying is occurring, I can arrange to catch Tony in the act. That way, Jamal won't have to tell on Tony. I'll also work with the playground supervisors and the boys' teacher to prevent further incidents. I'll talk with Tony's mom, too. I know her, and she'll be concerned about this."

"I'd also like both boys to have help in learning some new skills. Our school social worker has worked with some other bullying situations very effectively, so I'd like to have him spend some time with both Tony and Jamal. He might be just the male influence they both need."

"Those sound like some good ideas," Mrs. Watkins said. "If they don't work, I hope you will still consider removing Tony from the class."

"I never rule out any possibility, Mrs. Watkins," he replied.

Mrs. Watkins approached Mr. Brooks in a public place, when he was in the middle of making sure that the students safely boarded their buses. Mr. Brooks needed a few minutes to finish what he was doing, and he also wanted to move the conversation to a private and more appropriate location.

Mrs. Watkins came with a specific idea of what she wanted her son's principal to do. Mr. Brooks asked her explicitly what she wanted him to do. Her solution, removing the bully from Jamal's class, was an action that Mr. Watkins wouldn't think of doing, especially as a first attempt to solve the problem. Mr. Brooks explained his reasoning and outlined a plan of action. Mrs. Watkins was willing to cooperate and wait to see if it worked.

Welcome Anyone Who Approaches You to Air a Complaint

Even if an angry person bungles the communication with you, he has still given you a gift. It is an act of respect to address you directly, instead of gossiping to others or becoming passive-aggressive with you. Now the problem is out in the open where you can work with it.

Even in the ugliest interaction, you may still learn something important. Stay curious, and keep listening. You may gain valuable information about your staff, your students, or even yourself.

Chapter Summary

When someone initiates a difficult conversation with you, breathe deeply to calm yourself, keep your head clear, and slow down the velocity of the interaction. Work to not personalize what the other person is saying—this is a problem to be solved, not a test of who you are as a person. Stay curious and keep listening carefully to the other person. If necessary, move the conversation to a more appropriate setting. If the other person has managed to push your buttons and you are feeling highly reactive, ask for time.

During the conversation, try to preserve your working relationship with the other person. If you have had a negative impact on the other person, take responsibility and apologize. Wait to explain your intentions until you have taken responsibility for your impact. Find out what the other person wants you to do. If you cannot meet the request, offer other possibilities. Welcome anyone who comes to you personally to air a complaint. Consider it an act of respect to be approached directly, even if the person makes a mess of the rest of the interaction.

Chapter 9

Power Differentials in Difficult Conversations

When there is a power differential between the conversing parties, it is time to slow down and pay careful attention to the dynamics of the interaction. This chapter addresses difficult conversations initiated by both supervisors and supervisees. There is also a section in this chapter for union representatives to aid in determining when it would and would not be helpful to be present for such difficult conversations.

Initiating Difficult Conversations with Your Supervisees

When you are in a position of power and authority, your communications will usually be highly analyzed by those you supervise. Your every word may be studied to try to determine where the person stands with you. This is true if you are the superintendent, the principal, the director of special services, or the director of transportation. The other person will want to know if you respect his work, value his contribution, and care about his well-being.

You may even be treated to this level of scrutiny if you have a powerful position but are not responsible for hiring, evaluating, and firing people. Such informal power roles include department chairs, mentors, and union presidents, among others. People may still respond to you differently because of your position.

When you assume authority, many people will see you less clearly as a person. You will become a blank screen onto which they will project their unresolved authority issues. Such projection is not personal—any authority figure might get a similar response—but it can be challenging. If you are promoted from within the ranks of your peers to a supervisory position, many people will forget overnight that they trust you. You will become *them*, rather than *us*.

There will be days when you don't feel very powerful— you're coming down with a cold; you had a fight with your spouse that morning; or you're feeling anxious about your child's admission to college. Regardless of how you feel, others will still treat you as the authority. There are no time outs from formal leadership positions. If you try to sit on the bench, you will create a field of mistrust in your organization.

It is unreasonable to expect the people you lead to behave better than you do. What you do will set the tone for your individual and group interactions. If you are controlling, you will be met with control. If you are appeasing and don't stay current in dealing with problems, you will create a seething cauldron of unspoken resentments.

Yes, you do have that much impact as a leader. You can use your power as a tool for constructive change or as the catalyst for negativity and a toxic work environment. It's your choice. If you do not want to learn to use the power of your role in a responsible, trustworthy manner, you are misplaced in a leadership position.

Your responsibilities as a leader in difficult conversations are even greater. You must be very clear so that others know exactly what you mean. You need to model self-responsibility and management of your own reactivity, as well as sufficiency and compassion. It is essential that you give specific, accurate feedback to your supervisees about their impact, both positive and negative.

There are many circumstances that call for a supervisor to initiate a difficult conversation with a supervisee. We will examine three of them in detail: (1) addressing health and mental health issues that are affecting the workplace, (2) helping someone who is having difficulty adjusting to change, and (3) delivering bad news about a person's job.

Addressing Health and Mental Health Issues

When an employee's health or mental health status is causing a problem in the workplace, it is the responsibility of that person's supervisor to address the issue. The problem could be the employee's attendance or ability to perform her job adequately. The difficulty could also be in the amount of work time other employees are spending trying to help the person who is ill.

Compassionate limit setting is the solution. You may care deeply about the well-being of a supervisee and still need to set limits on her behavior. In preparing for this conversation, you will want to consider the welfare of the person in question, the impact on her coworkers, and whether the work is getting accomplished.

Setting limits on behavior stemming from health or mental health concerns is a disciplinary conversation, so it is important that you confine yourself to discussing work-related behaviors. What your employees choose to do with their time outside of work is not your business and should not enter into this conversation. You are not simply one friend talking to another friend about her health—you are acting from your position of authority over the other person.

> Jack was the district transportation director. His office was in the bus garage, and he supervised the drivers, mechanics, and a pool of five female secretaries who attended

to the details of moving students around the district. Over the past three months, Jack had noticed that the pool was getting increasingly little work done. He also saw that Candace, one of the secretaries, was becoming disturbingly thin, spending a great deal of time in the bathroom, not looking well, and missing more and more work each month.

When Candace called in sick one day, the other four secretaries came together to talk to Jack. They told him that they had walked in on Candace in the bathroom several times as she was throwing up her lunch. She had confessed that she was bulimic, that she repeatedly ate huge quantities of junk food, and that she purged so she wouldn't gain weight. They knew that Candace lived alone and had few friends and no family, so they felt responsible for her. They told Jack that they were very worried about Candace and wanted to enlist him in trying to help her.

Jack responded, "I appreciate your coming to me with your concerns about Candace. I can see why you are so worried about her. Bulimia is a very serious disorder. I'm very concerned, too. I promise you that I will assist Candace in getting the help she needs outside of the office."

"What I would like from you four ladies is to stop focusing on Candace and her problems. Because we are work colleagues, we are not the ones who can solve her problems. It violates Candace's privacy and takes your minds off of your work. During work time, I want you to put your attention back on your work."

One of the secretaries replied, "We haven't been doing as much work lately because we've been so focused on Candace. I think it would be great if you could get some help for Candace, but how will we know if she's all right?"

"We might not know how she is doing," said Jack. "All I can do is make sure that she gets a quality referral; I can't make her participate. We're just going to have to live with that because it's the only appropriate thing we can do. If we intrude on her private life, we will just be compounding the problem. I know that it's hard to both care and accept the limits of what you can do." The women reluctantly agreed to try Jack's plan.

Jack's next step was to have a private conversation with Candace. He booked a room in another building so that they could have the conversation away from the other four secretaries. Jack started off the conversation: "Candace, I'm concerned about you. I don't know what's going on, and it's not my business. What is my concern is that you have been missing a great deal of work, so much so that you are almost out of sick days. When you are here, you are frequently not at your desk. When you're not here, other people have to do your job, and that's not okay."

"As your supervisor, I want you to be at work and at your desk. I also don't want whatever is going on in your life to become an office problem that other people spend time trying to solve. That would be disrespectful to you and inappropriate in the workplace."

Candace interjected, "Jack, I'm bulimic. I thought I had it under control, but I guess I don't. I keep telling myself that I will stop binging and purging, but I can't do it. I'm scared."

"I'm worried about you, too, Candace," replied Jack. "I would guess that bulimia is something you can't shake without professional help. The district has an excellent employee assistance program. It's confidential, and I know several people who have found the counselors to be very helpful. If you need a referral to a physician or a mental health professional, they could help you find the right person."

"However you decide to deal with your bulimia, it's important that you move it outside of the workplace. I'll support you in any appropriate way."

Candace nodded and said, "I'll talk to the employee assistance people today. It's time."

Jack had to field a two-part problem. First, he had to set a limit on the four secretaries who were spending too much of their work time trying to solve Candace's problem. He explained the proper workplace boundaries and set an appropriate limit on their behavior. He also coached them to let go of the outcome and let them know that they would not be updated on

Candace's situation. Jack acknowledged the genuine concern that the women had for Candace and let them know that he cared, too. He found the balance between caring and setting limits.

Then Jack met with Candace in a location that did not feed the over-involvement of the other secretaries. Jack stuck to his concerns about Candace's performance in the first part of the conversation. He did not attempt to intrude on Candace's privacy or diagnose her problem. He also avoided forming an unproductive triangle by not referring to his conversation with her colleagues. When Candace chose to reveal her bulimia, Jack was ready with a referral to the employee assistance program.

Jack concluded his conversation with Candace by reiterating his insistence that she show up at the office and do her own work. In the future, Jack will need to continue to monitor Candace's performance. If it does not improve, he will have to take further corrective action and will want to consult the district's attorney before doing so. It will not be appropriate for him to attempt to counsel Candace himself or to give her much more attention about her bulimia. To do so might feed the problem.

Taking Corrective Action with an Employee

An effective leader steps in to take corrective action when an employee is behaving inappropriately or not performing well. Early intervention provides the employee with an opportunity to resolve the problem before it becomes a threat to her job or a serious threat to the people she serves.

It is not an act of kindness on the part of a supervisor to ignore problem behavior until it escalates to the point of crisis. When this happens, the supervisor is not protecting the employee, but is merely avoiding doing something difficult. Leaders who do not take corrective action when it is needed are not respected by their employees or by the community that they serve.

Anita was the principal of a suburban elementary school with rapidly changing demographics. In two years, the students had gone from all white and upper middle-class to a mixture that included immigrants from five different language groups. Most of the teachers had risen to the challenge of the new diversity, but a few were struggling to make the change.

Anita was particularly concerned about Ruth, a fourth-grade teacher with over 20 years of experience in the district. Anita had heard Ruth talk repeatedly about "grieving" for the homogeneous days when teaching was "easier." Anita's apprehension escalated when a parent reported that Ruth had referred to the immigrant parents of her students as "those lazy foreigners." Anita decided that it was time to have a difficult conversation with Ruth."

When Ruth came for their meeting, Anita began the conversation by saying, "Ruth, for many years I could count you among the top five teachers in our building. You know that you have been highly regarded by students, parents, and your colleagues. I'm concerned about the erosion in your success that I've noticed since our students have become more diverse."

"Here's what I'm seeing. I have more discipline reports from you than from any other teacher in the building—all on immigrant students. Parents have stopped requesting you as a teacher, and a few have specifically asked that their children not be in your class next year. Ruth, I'm very concerned about all of this, and I'd like to hear what you have to say about it."

Ruth looked down at her feet and replied, "I don't like all of the changes in our district. The children used to be prepared to learn fourth-grade material. Their parents wanted to be involved. Now, these foreign parents don't care about whether their children do their homework or are respectful."

Anita queried, "Ruth, what makes you think that the immigrant parents don't care?"

Ruth responded, "When I send notes about bad behavior home with the students, the parents don't even bother to respond. Bad grades don't even get their attention."

Anita said, "Many of the immigrant parents don't read English. Your notes probably mystify them. You seem to be mistaking a communications gap for lack of interest."

"That may be true," Ruth countered, "but what are they doing in my class in the first place. Why can't you put them in a special class where they won't disrupt everything?"

"You know that's not what our district has decided," Anita replied. "Our plan, based on research and the experience of many other districts, is to mainstream all of our newcomers and offer them additional support services. You don't like the plan. You don't want things to change. I'm not faulting you for how you feel."

"I do need you to deal with your feelings and get past your resentment. You must adapt your teaching skills so that you can be successful with all of our students and their parents, not just the familiar ones. I also don't want you making any more disparaging remarks about the parents of any of your students."

Ruth folded her arms and exclaimed, "Maybe I should transfer to one of the other schools in our district that is still like it used to be!"

"Ruth, this is just the beginning," answered Anita. "We have a declining enrollment in our district. The only way we can maintain our student population is by welcoming immigrants into our community. They can pick anywhere they want to live. If we can't welcome them and figure out how to communicate with them, they will choose other communities. You can transfer now, but you will soon be faced with the same situation in all of the schools in our district."

Ruth sighed, "Alright, Anita, what do you want me to do?"

Anita answered, "First, tell me what you think might help you."

"A full-time teacher's aide would make a big difference," said Ruth.

"I don't have the funds for that, but what I can do," said Anita, "is get you some blocks of time with the cultural liaisons from each of the immigrant groups. They can help you communicate with the parents."

"I'd also like for you to participate in the upcoming training that the diversity coordinator has planned. It will give you in-depth understanding of each of the ethnic groups and help you to adapt your teaching strategies to work with them. Are you willing?"

"I don't think I have much choice," Ruth said.

Anita concluded, "Ruth, I have faith in your ability to adapt your skills to work in our changed environment. I also know that you can only do that if you accept the situation and adopt a more positive attitude. It's your choice."

Anita addressed Ruth's attitude, her behavior, and her skill set. They all needed adjusting. Anita was not successful in changing Ruth's attitude in this initial conversation, but she did put limits on her behavior and insisted that she update her teaching proficiencies. She also insisted that Ruth participate in diversity training, which Anita hoped would help Ruth to improve her attitude. Finally, Anita offered Ruth help from cultural liaisons who could assist in communicating with immigrant parents and provide Ruth with insights into the home lives of her students.

Anita will need to continue to pay close attention to Ruth's mind-set and her interactions with her students and their parents. Anita has no control over Ruth's point of view about immigrants, but she does have jurisdiction over the impact of Ruth's behavior in the workplace. If Ruth cannot bring herself to a more respectful, competent place with the newcomers, Anita will have to take further, decisive action.

Delivering Bad News to an Employee

One of the hardest parts of leadership is delivering bad news to an employee. The dreaded tidings may be that a loved one has died, a promotion is being denied, funding has been cut, or disciplinary action is being taken.

One of the most difficult things to do is to fire an employee. When you have to fire someone, all of the principles of successful difficult conversations still apply. It is your responsibility to be respectful and compassionate, no matter what the person has done.

When you are delivering bad news, it is not appropriate to blame a third party. To do so would form an unproductive triangle, with you as the rescuer and whoever made the decision as the villain. For example, if you are a principal and the school board has eliminated funding for the extracurricular program of one of your teachers, it would not be suitable to say, "Those jerks on the school board voted down your funding." It is fitting to say, "The funding for your program has been cut. I know it's a big disappointment, and I'm sorry."

Whenever you have something very hard to say, begin with the bad news. If you lead with anything else, the other person will not hear it—he will simply be steeling himself for what is to come. Anything else you have to say to the person should come afterwards.

> Tom was a high school principal who needed to fire Brad, a first-year chemistry teacher. Brad had been suspended from his job after he hit a student while supervising in the cafeteria. Tom asked Brad to come to his office at the end of a school day.
>
> When they sat down together, Tom began, "Brad, I am firing you as of now. I'll take you to your classroom when we're finished talking so that you can get your personal belongings. You will not be allowed to come back onto school grounds, and you will be expected to have no contact with the student you hit."
>
> Brad slumped in his chair and began to cry. "Being a teacher wasn't like I thought it would be—thirsty minds soaking up knowledge. All year I felt like the students were in charge, not me. I finally just lost it in the cafeteria and decked that boy. I've never hit anyone before in my life. In fact, I was the nerdy kid that always got picked on. I don't know what I'm going to do now."
>
> "Brad," Tom said gently, "you seem like a very bright guy. When I observed your classes, I was struck by your passion for chemistry. Maybe the teaching part was just not right for you. You might want to look for a job that is not so people focused."

Tom was straightforward with Brad. Tom fired Brad and set clear limits. Then Tom listened to Brad with compassion and provided useful feedback for Brad's next professional effort. If

Tom had reversed the order of what he had to say to Tom, his good advice would probably have been lost in Tom's anxiety to find out if he was going to be fired. At no point did Tom shame or judge Brad.

Initiating a Difficult Conversation with Your Supervisor

If you make it through your entire career as an educator without needing to initiate a difficult conversation with your supervisor, you will have had a highly unusual work life. Because supervisors are human, they make their share of mistakes. When you think that your supervisor's behavior or failure to act has had a negative impact on you, it's time to initiate a difficult conversation.

If you are conflict averse, it is tempting to use the power differential between you and your supervisor as an excuse to avoid the conversation—"I couldn't say that because he might fire me" or "If I told him what I really think, he would get back at me in some way." These are just fancy ways of saying, "I lack the courage to have this conversation, and I'm going to hang the blame on my boss."

Supervisors are no better at mind reading than the average person. If you don't tell yours what's really bothering you, he won't have a clue and won't be able to do anything about it. Whatever he did or did not do is likely to recur, and you will feel even more irritated.

It's not fair to remain silent with your supervisor and complain about him to someone else. By third-partying you move into victim mode, compound the problem, and dishonor your supervisor and yourself. If the person you turn to is a work colleague, you have also helped to erode the trust level in your workplace.

Everything that you have learned while reading this book applies to initiating a difficult conversation with your supervisor. You are most likely to have a successful conversation if you prepare yourself for the conversation. When you sit down with your supervisor, you will want to be respectful and collaborative, rather than going into victim mode and becoming accusatory.

Don't treat your supervisor like the enemy. Approach him like you would want to be treated. If you have difficulty with authority, manage your reactivity before you initiate the difficult conversation. The fact that he reminds you of your father is not his problem. Be specific, don't resort to blaming or shaming, and ask for what you want. Remain flexible and creative, and try to find a win/win solution.

> Rita, a middle school art teacher, was angry with her principal, Doug. After she had calmed down and prepared herself for the conversation, she scheduled a meeting with him.
>
> Rita began the conversation with, "Doug, I'll get right to the point—I didn't like the way you responded to my scheduling ideas in our staff meeting on Monday. You said that my plan was 'half-baked.' I'm not asking you to adopt my plan; I just want you to treat my thinking with respect. I put a great deal of thought into that proposal. You may not have liked it, but you didn't need to be derisive."
>
> Doug responded defensively, "Well it was a dumb idea!"
>
> "Doug, you're doing it again—you just called my idea 'dumb.' I don't like it. Again, I'm not asking you to like or accept my plan."
>
> Doug countered, "Aren't you being a little thin-skinned?"
>
> Rita struggled to hold her ground and said, "Doug, I want to have a good working relationship with you. When you use language that is derogatory toward me, I feel disrespected. If you do it in front of the whole faculty, I feel humiliated."
>
> "Okay," said Doug, "I think I get it. I think this is the same thing my wife's been trying to tell me. You want me to use different language when I disagree with you, so that you will know that I am talking about your ideas and not about you. Is that it?"
>
> "Yes," replied Rita.
>
> "Good," said Doug, "I can do that. I do respect you, you know."

Rita's concern about Doug's language may seem mundane or not worth the risk of a difficult conversation with her principal. It is this very kind of small irritant that can erode a working relationship over time if it is not addressed. The fact that Rita felt disrespected was enough to warrant a difficult conversation.

Rita had to persist with Doug, who, in their conversation, kept repeating the same type of behavior about which she was complaining. She did not personalize his response and tried to rephrase her concerns so that he would understand.

Doug clearly had a blind spot about his unproductive use of language in disagreements over ideas. Rita gave him the gift of feedback about his impact on her. Fortunately, Doug connected her comments to a complaint he had received from his wife. If he is wise, Doug will accept this input about an unproductive behavior pattern and take corrective action. If he drops the disrespectful use of language with Rita, he will create a strong bond of trust with her. If continues to use derisive language with Rita, he will be giving her a double message: "I say I respect you, but I don't act like it."

The Union Representative's Role in Difficult Conversations

To be effective as a union official, it is important for you to intervene on behalf of employees in a way that is constructive and does not add to the problem. It is appropriate for a union representative to accompany a teacher to a disciplinary hearing. It is not productive for the union person to have a difficult conversation for a teacher. Your role is to make sure that the contract is followed, not to be a crutch.

When a teacher is uncomfortable with conflict and has a problem with her principal, it is tempting to prevail upon the union steward to go and speak for her. If the union representative plays this role, an unproductive triangle is formed—with the teacher in the victim role, the principal in the villain role, and the union person as rescuer. The teacher will be reinforced in her notion that she cannot handle conflict. The principal will feel frustrated because he has not been able to talk directly with the person with the problem. The union representative will either feel used and in the middle or get a false high from being a white knight. The working relationship between the principal and the building representative will be tarnished, and trust will be eroded between them.

Inserting the union where it does not belong may create an adversarial situation. The minute you walk in the door for or with a member, the tenor of the conversation changes. What might have been a simple conversation between employee and employer is now a big deal.

It is not your job to try to keep every union member happy all of the time by doing anything that they ask of you. If you cannot say "no" or you have a strong history of being a rescuer, being a building representative or a union president may not be a useful place for you to serve. Pick a different role in the union, one in which you will not be asked repeatedly to be a rescuer. Alternatively, use these challenging positions to practice saying "no" and keeping appropriate boundaries to avoid joining unproductive triangles.

To avoid getting caught in having a difficult conversation for a member, a union representative must know when and how to say "no." Here are some questions for the union representative that will help to sort out when to agree and when to decline.

- Is this a general policy issue, a disciplinary situation, or a personal problem that the teacher has with the principal?
- What would be the impact on me if I did what the teacher is asking? On the principal? On the teacher? On the union? On our working relationships?
- Will I form an unproductive triangle with me as the rescuer if I go and talk to the principal?
- Is this a recurring pattern with this teacher to want someone else to speak for her?
- Is there any real reason why the teacher cannot go directly to the principal herself?

- Am I about to agree to this request simply because I can't say "no" or because I want to be a hero?
- How can I coach the teacher to have the conversation herself?
- Can I let go of the outcome if I say "no" and the teacher does not choose to have the conversation?

The following conversation shows a union representative using his skills effectively.

Joe was the teachers' union representative for his elementary school building, where Dan was the principal. A kindergarten teacher, Madge, approached Joe for assistance, saying, "Joe, I need the union to help me. Did you see the room assignments for next year? Dan gave me the room with the tiny windows again. I just can't stand being in there another year, especially in the winter. I come to work in the dark, work in a gloomy room, and then go home in the dark. It's depressing." Madge stopped and looked at Joe expectantly.

"I'm not sure what you're asking me to do, Madge."

"I want you to talk to Dan for me and get me a different room for next year."

Joe responded, "I can see why you wouldn't want that room every year. This seems like a conversation you should have with Dan yourself."

"Dan doesn't like me," replied Madge.

"What gives you that idea?"

"I speak to him in the halls, and most of the time he just acts as if I'm not there. I don't know what I've ever done to him, but he won't even give me the time of day. His sticking me with this room every year is proof he has it in for me."

"Madge, I've worked with Dan a great deal as the building rep. My impression of him is that he is a mixed bag. On the one hand, he can be oblivious to the point of rudeness. That's not such a good quality in a principal, but it's not personal. His head is just somewhere else. On the other hand, Dan is very open to feedback, even when it's difficult. He does make the occasional mess, but he cleans it up. I suggest that you not take Dan personally and go and talk with him."

"Oh, Joe, I couldn't do that. You have such a strong relationship with Dan, and I hate conflict."

"Madge, you've been teaching for a long time. Surely you've had a number of difficult conversations with principals."

"Oh, no, I have never challenged a principal. Not once." Joe looked at Madge incredulously, and she continued, "When I was a child, I was punished if I ever complained, so you see why I just can't do it. Can't you please take care of this for me? Judith used to go to bat for me when she was the building rep. Isn't this why we elected you?"

Joe replied, "I think that's a common misconception—that the union person is supposed to be a wedge between the teachers and the principal so that the teachers never have to face the principal when they don't like something. That's not my role. I'm here to see that the administration follows the rules of the contract with teachers. I accompany members to disciplinary hearings, and I work with Dan to resolve policy issues that affect the whole staff. In my union role, I do not speak for individual teachers when they have a beef with Dan."

"What I could do is coach you about how to talk with Dan about changing rooms. We could even do a role-play, and I could be Dan so you can practice. I have faith in both you and Dan that you can work this out together."

"No, Joe, I'll just bring in some lamps to get more light in my room."

"It's your choice, Madge. By the way, have you talked with the other kindergarten teachers about the possibility of rotating rooms every year so no one gets stuck with the small windows every year?"

"Oh, no, I don't want any conflict with them either," replied Madge.

Madge tried several different ways to make Joe feel guilty so that he would have her difficult conversation with Dan for her: accusing him of not doing his elected job, referring to her difficult childhood, comparing him with a previous building representative, complimenting his working relationship with Dan, and sounding pathetic about bringing in lamps. It was all a sophisticated victim mode response, and Madge was trying to get Joe to rescue her from Dan, the villain.

Joe was able to decline Madge's request and thus stay out of an unproductive triangle with Dan and her. He explained his role clearly and offered Madge another alternative—coaching and role-playing. Joe let go of the outcome, even though he guessed that Madge would continue to seethe and would probably complain about him to other teachers. He knew that these things were out of his control.

Chapter Summary

When the two parties in a difficult conversation do not have equal power in an organization, there are additional dynamics to attend to in the exchange. The issues are somewhat different, depending on who initiates the conversation, the supervisor or the employee. The dynamics also change if a union representative plays a role.

If a supervisor initiates the conversation, he needs to pay special attention to his impact on the other person. He should try to be compassionate, avoid being judgmental, and try to give clear and consistent messages to the employee.

In addressing health and mental health issues, a supervisor must address work-related behavior and not try to be a counselor. It is imperative that supervisors initiate difficult conversations when an employee is not performing well so that the person has an opportunity to correct the problem. When a supervisor has to do the difficult job of firing someone, it works best to deliver the bad news at the beginning of the conversation because that is what the employee will be waiting to hear.

When an employee initiates a difficult conversation with her supervisor, the most effective approach is to be direct and not accusatory. Any tendency to move into victim mode needs to be managed before engaging with the supervisor. It's not fair to dodge the conversation and complain to others.

Union presidents and building representatives will be asked to have difficult conversations for their members. If they agree, they will form unproductive triangles with the members and the administration, and it will impede the genuinely useful roles that they need to play in enforcing contractual agreements.

Chapter 10

Keys to Success

This chapter pulls together key concepts presented through-out this book. First we examine important distinctions that will help you to be more effective in difficult conversations. Then, we look at the best ways to prevent conflict. Finally, we investigate the factors that are most likely to lead to successful difficult conversations.

Key Distinctions

Understanding some key distinctions helps you to communicate more effectively and to be a more constructive participant in difficult conversations.

Intention vs. Impact

Your intention is what you mean to accomplish with your words and actions. Your impact is the effect that your words and actions actually have on the other person. It is possible to have the best of intentions but still have a negative impact. You are responsible for both your intention and your impact. If you do not have the impact that you intended, it is up to you to set things right with the other person. People will not be very interested in your intentions unless you take responsibility for your impact. It's not enough to say, "That's not the way I meant it." In a successful difficult conversation, both parties address their intentions and their impact.

Reactivity vs. Proactivity

Reactivity is a knee-jerk response to what is coming at you from the outside. Emotional reactivity is a heightened state that makes clear thinking difficult. If you are angry and reactive, you are likely to act on your ire in an unproductive way. When you are in a reactive state, you will not be a reliable participant in a difficult conversation. Take the time to collect yourself before proceeding.

Proactivity is the act of taking charge of yourself and your emotional reactions in a dynamic way. When you are proactive, you do not wait for others to act and then respond; you formulate your own plan of action in consultation with others. In a state of emotional arousal, the proactive person manages his feelings rather than taking them out on others. Proactivity helps you to prevent conflict and is an effective strategy for resolving difficult situations.

Making Assumptions vs. Checking In

Assumptions are what you think might be true for another person. They are your opinions about what the other person is thinking and about the hidden meaning behind his or her words and actions. Assumptions are not facts. You are responsible for your assumptions. Acting on unchecked assumptions is disrespectful and leads to conflict. For a difficult conversation to be successful, it is essential that both parties air and check all of their assumptions about each other.

Checking in with another person about the correct interpretation of his or her words and actions is an act of respect and is the only way to obtain accurate information. Checking in helps prevent conflict.

Bonding with Fear vs. Managing Fear

Focusing on your fears makes them stronger. You can find many sophisticated reasons to bond with fear and avoid a difficult conversation. These excuses are simply weak-hearted artful dodges.

- If I tell him what I think, he won't like me anymore.
- I don't want to hurt her feelings.
- I wouldn't know what to say.
- She couldn't handle it.
- He won't listen anyway.
- I'd rather keep the peace by keeping my feelings to myself.
- I feel intimidated by her, so I would never question her.
- I pick my battles, and this isn't one of them.

It is natural to feel fear in unfamiliar, challenging situations. It is your responsibility to manage your fear and not let it control you. Don't mistake your fear of conflict for a legitimate reason to avoid difficult conversations.

Focus on your goals and your vision for your workplace rather than on your fears. The poet Audre Lorde said, "When I dare to be powerful—to use my strength in the service of my vision, then it becomes less and less important whether I am afraid."

Role Responsibility vs. Personal Responsibility

In any organization there are named leaders who have clear responsibilities because of their roles. That being said, everyone in the organization is responsible for creating a positive atmosphere and healthy working conditions. Every seat in the workplace is a position of personal leadership. It is not fair to abdicate your personal responsibility and expect your managers and supervisors to carry the whole load. A handful of leaders cannot create an exciting, vibrant workplace—to do so requires the full participation of everyone in the group.

Language of Inclusion vs. Language of Separation

The language you use in resolving conflicts may make the difference between whether you have a successful or an unsuccessful conversation. The goal is to include the ideas of both parties, rather than to make one person right and the other person wrong. For the greatest effectiveness, make sure that your language reflects both/and, rather than either/or thinking. Build on the ideas of others, rather than simply competing with them.

Using the word "but" can bring a productive conversation to a screeching halt—"I liked your presentation to the staff, *but* I disagree with one of your key points." The word "but" cancels out anything positive you have said first and implies that the compliment was just sugar coating. Substituting the word "and" has a completely different impact—"I liked your presentation to the staff, *and* I disagree with one of your key points." The word "and" invites further discussion.

Inner Critic vs. Curiosity

The inner critic is harsh and is not based in reality. It is the voice of insufficiency. You must choose whether you listen to its lies or not. If you allow your self-critic to control your inner life, you will be unreliable in your interactions with colleagues because you will view everything through the fog of self-doubt and blame. When the inner critic is in charge, you will not be able to receive feedback about your impact, positive or negative, and you will be unable to correct course when necessary. You will feel bad about yourself, and you will find it difficult to trust yourself, others, or the circumstances.

The alternative to the inner critic is the voice of curiosity. When you can remain curious, even in the face of challenging people and situations, you will be better able to maintain your sense of self and to act with integrity. Curiosity requires that you not rush to judgment, but remain open to receiving information. It allows you to be flexible and to maintain a fresh perspective. Curiosity is required if you want to find creative solutions to problems.

Compassion vs. Judgment

Compassion is the quality of having open hearted empathy for others. It is possible to maintain your compassion, even if you don't like others or their behavior. If you close your heart, any attempt to have a difficult conversation will be felt as mean-spirited or false. Even people who are angry and disgruntled respond well to genuine compassion. Closed heartedness is also stressful to you physically and emotionally. You suffer more than others when your compassion fails.

Making judgments about others is what happens when you have a failure of compassion. When you close your heart, you are more likely to develop a fixed negative perspective of others that will not give them room to reach a meeting of the minds with you. Even when you do not speak your judgment, it is felt by others and then creates a chasm between you and the person you are judging.

Collegiality vs. Appeasement

Being a good colleague does not mean that you have to accept unproductive behavior without comment—to do so is appeasement. A capable colleague is honest with others without being shaming or blaming. It is not respectful to your colleague to let him get away with conduct that is harmful to you or to the organization. Appeasement is lack of courage dressed up to look like peacemaking.

Person vs. Behavior

When you don't like what someone is doing or saying, it is important to distinguish between his behavior and his identity as a person. Address the problematic conduct, without questioning someone's personal identity. Behavior may be a manifestation of character, but other people's core selves are their business, not yours. Don't expect a good reaction if you attack another person's identity. You wouldn't like it either. It is constructive to say, "I feel disrespected when you talk to me in that tone of voice." It would be inappropriate to say, "You're such a bully—you always go for the jugular when you disagree with me."

Contribution vs. Blame

It's easy to fall into the trap of wanting troublesome situations to be someone else's fault. Usually, problems are co-created by all of the parties. The most disarming thing you can do in trying to resolve a conflict is to acknowledge your own contribution to the problem and then to invite others to join you. Teasing out how we have all contributed to a problem feels very different from being accused and blamed.

Respect vs. Fixed Perspective

Respect is the willingness to look again. If you are not willing to remain open to possibility, it will be very difficult for you to be a constructive participant in a difficult conversation. If you have already made up your mind, you have a fixed perspective, and you will be unable to work with others to solve problems. In other words, you have to let go of being right to have a successful difficult conversation. If you are right and others are wrong, you cannot find win/win solutions together.

Keys to Preventing Conflict

Difficult conversations can be used to prevent conflict and to resolve conflict. Prevention is always preferable to remediation. The following are key ways to avert major discord.

Say What You Mean

Let others know where you stand. Say what's on your mind without blaming, judging, or shaming others or yourself. Do your best to avoid giving double messages to others. What comes out of your mouth should be congruent with your values.

Go Directly to the Source

If you have a problem with another person's behavior, go directly to that person and address your concerns. Be specific. Give examples. If you turn to a third person instead, you will create both conflict and an unproductive triangle.

Stay Current

When you need to have a courageous conversation with someone, do it within one week. If you hold yourself to this standard, you will prevent stress, preserve your working relationship with the other person, and keep small problems from becoming large ones. Giving yourself a deadline for speaking up will help you to get past your fears.

Do What You Say

When you have made a commitment, keep your word. If you need to amend your promise, do so clearly and in a timely manner. Make your actions match your words to preserve your integrity and build trust with yourself and others.

Take Responsibility for Your Intentions and Your Impact

Consider your motives before you act. When in doubt, don't act; wait for clarity before taking action. Notice whether you have the impact you intended. Ask for feedback. If you have a negative impact, take responsibility. Make amends, and work to not repeat the behavior in the future. If you do not take responsibility for your impact, you will cause hurt and harm and will cast yourself in the role of villain in your organization.

Give Others Feedback about Their Impact on You

The only way others can take corrective action is if they know that they have created a problem. Feedback delivered without blame or judgment is a great gift to give to another person.

Be equally willing to give positive feedback to those around you. Let people know when they have had a positive impact on you. Without this information, others will often assume the worst—that you don't like them, appreciate them, or value their work. Harness the power of acknowledgement. Let people know where they stand with you.

Listen Deeply

First, it is important to listen to yourself. Know what you think about important issues so that you can act from your own sense of things rather than being other-directed. Pay attention to your feelings, and harness the information that they provide. Listen to your heart to learn what is most important to you and then act on that information.

It is equally important to listen deeply to others. When you are talking with someone, give that person your undivided attention. Be fully present. Set aside your fixed views, and be open to possibility. Be willing to be changed by what you hear from others. Look for what you have in common—it will usually be far greater than your disagreements—and build on it.

Check Your Assumptions

You will be tempted to make assumptions when you do not have enough information. It is easy to make an assumption and then treat it as if it were a fact. When you realize that you are about to make an assumption about another person, do her the courtesy of asking for the missing information instead. Mind reading is disrespectful and usually inaccurate. Acting on unchecked assumptions creates conflict.

Make Tasks Explicit within the Work Group

Tasks will go smoothly when all of the following are clear to everyone: what you are trying to accomplish and why, who is responsible for each part of the task, what the deadlines are for each segment, and how the success of the project will be determined. Having joint clarity about each of these pieces of information allows for accountability and a feeling of achievement once the tasks are completed. A lack of clarity about tasks leads to confusion, inefficiency, failure, and conflict.

Say "No" When You Need to Do So

If you don't want to do something, don't agree to do it. The ability to say "no" is part of having good boundaries with others. You have to be willing to disappoint other people sometimes in order to preserve your own sense of self. There will be many times when you have a legitimate conflict of interest with what others want from you. If you give in and do what is not right for you, your resentment will come out in some way and will lead to conflict.

Support Others Instead of Trying to Fix or Rescue Them

The only person you can change is yourself. Often, others will modify their behavior in response to the changes you make in yourself. Taking responsibility for your own mistakes by changing your behavior is one of the most powerful and inspiring things you can do.

When other adults come to you for help, give only that assistance which will empower them. Do not listen to their repeated complaints about others, take sides with them, or attempt to act for them. Those responses will put you in the rescuer role and will create an unproductive triangle.

Create Value for Yourself at Work

You are responsible for your own happiness on the job. Create opportunities to use your gifts and talents instead of waiting for others to invite you to do so. Through your own words and actions, work to create trust and a positive work environment. If you see a problem, bring it forward with at least three possible solutions.

Make a Place for Everyone in the Organization

Work to include everyone, especially the people with whom you disagree or think you don't like. Harness your differences to gain a broader perspective. Don't expect everyone to be like you. Do not write off anyone in the organization. You may have to set limits on some people's behavior at the same time that you safeguard their places in the group. If you indulge in exclusion or scapegoating, you will create a field of mistrust in your organization.

Make Organizational Agreements about How You Will Treat Each Other

As a group, agree on a clear set of standards for how you will conduct your business with each other. Hold yourselves accountable for sticking to these agreements. How you treat each other will determine your organizational climate. The better your workplace environment, the more productive and creative you will be together and the more satisfied you will be individually.

Keys to Successful Difficult Conversations

The principles of preventing conflict also apply to resolving conflict. The following are other factors to consider in having successful difficult conversations.

When Possible, Prepare Yourself for the Conversation

Some difficult conversations will occur on the spot. For others, you will have the luxury of preparing yourself for interaction ahead of time. When you can prepare, think about what has prompted the need for the conversation. Determine how you are feeling about the other person and about yourself. Assess the core of your concerns, and think of illustrative examples.

Ascertain the impact that the other person has had on you in the circumstances of concern as well as your own impact on the other person. Check your intentions toward the other person and any assumptions you may have. Figure out what you want from the other person to resolve the issue and what it will take for you to feel successful about your own part of the interaction. Prepare yourself thoroughly, rather than rehearsing, so that you can be fully present in the difficult conversation.

When You Have a Concern, Address It

If another person's behavior has had a negative impact on you, have a difficult conversation with him within one week. Invite him to solve the problem with you, and acknowledge your own part in the situation. Provide feedback to the other person about his impact on you, and invite him to give you similar information. Distinguish between your intentions and your impact. Be constructive, and avoid shaming, blaming, judging, and using inflammatory language. Account for tasks and also tend to your working relationship with the other person. Check all of your assumptions about each other. Find out what each of you wants in order to resolve the situation.

Develop Your Capacity to Respond When Others Initiate Difficult Conversations

You may find that others approach you with velocity when they are disgruntled. Be grateful when someone comes to you directly, even if he is inelegant in his presentation of the problem. If necessary, move the conversation to a more appropriate venue. Remember to keep breathing, and try not to personalize what he says to you. If you are feeling highly reactive, ask to meet with him at a later time. If you realize that you have had a negative impact on the other person, intentionally or unintentionally, apologize. Acknowledge your impact on the other person before letting him know what your intention was. Keep listening to him, and ask him what, if anything, he wants you to do. If you cannot meet his request, offer several other options.

Let Go of the Outcome

It is an illusion to think that you have control over the outcome of a difficult conversation. If you enter the dialogue with an agenda for a specific result, you are likely to engage in various forms of controlling behavior to accomplish your goal. You might attempt to manipulate the situation or the other person. Control will not bring a positive result, even if you get your way.

The alternative is to let go of the outcome. Enter the conversation with an idea of what you would like to have happen. Then remain attentive, and work together with the other person to find a win/win resolution. If the two of you work together collaboratively, your combined creativity will produce solutions that neither one of you could have found on your own.

Talk It Out!

There is no one right way to have a difficult conversation. It's a messy process at best. The most important thing is that you find the courage to say what's on your mind. When you dare to speak from your heart, you will build your sense of sufficiency, increase your personal happiness, and help to create a workplace environment where trust, creativity, and learning can flourish.